DON'T BUY THE BULL

DON'T BUY THE BULL

By Cassandra Toroian

DON'T BUY THE BULL

Dispelling Disastrous Investment Advice and Money-Myths in Our New Economy

By Cassandra Toroian

STERLING & ROSS PUBLISHERS

NEW YORK

Published by
Sterling & Ross Publishers
New York, NY 10001
www.sterlingandross.com

Library of Congress Cataloging-in-Publication Data

Toroian, Cassandra.
Don't buy the bull : dispelling disastrous investment advice and
money-myths in our new economy / by Cassandra Toroian.
p. cm.
Includes bibliographical references and index.
ISBN 978-0-9821392-6-4 (hbk.)
1. Investments. 2. Finance, Personal. I. Title.
HG4521.T665 2010
332.6--dc22
2010001330

ISBN: 978-0-9821392-6-4

Cover design by The Book Designers
Book design by Rachel Trusheim

10 9 8 7 6 5 4 3 2 1

Printed in the United States of America.

This book is dedicated to my family:
Jackie, Mom, and Dad.

ACKNOWLEGDMENTS

In many ways this book was 10 years in the making. I always knew I had a book inside me, it was just a matter of finding it and pulling it out. Thank you to Colleen and Carol for the snowy car ride discussion of our common dislike of "personal finance gurus." You were true muses. Thank you, Jackie, for agreeing that we should help two strangers who needed help. That experience gave me the energy to write this book. Your generosity in always keeping my world orderly and sane gave me the time to write this. Thank you, Mom and Dad, for always believing in me. You have never once laughed at my light-bulb moments. Thanks to Drew Nederpelt, who actually answered my "cold call" e-mail and was willing to take the chance on me and my anti-guru concept. And thanks to Rachel Trusheim, Nadina Persaud, Jamie Metrick, Melissa Darcey, Maryann Yin, Terese Kerrigan, and everyone at Sterling & Ross Publishers.

TABLE OF CONTENTS

Myth #14: It's OK to use PMI.

Myth #15: Never lease a car.

Myth #16: Interest-only mortgages are insane.

Chapter 5: Life & Money Decisions   101

Myth #17: Never borrow using an adjustable rate loan.

Myth #18: Never marry anyone who insists on a prenup.

Myth #19: The $100 a month you give to your kids for little indulgences is not worth it— buy a life insurance policy instead.

Myth #20: Parents should always put their own financial health before their children's education.

Myth #21: Cosigning on a loan is OK to help someone out.

Myth #22: Helping others and giving to charity is always a wonderful and fulfilling experience.

Myth #23: You can do all this on your own.

INTRODUCTION

Ibelieve in life paths. We all have a path to follow—
the question is not that the path exists, but whether
we choose to follow it. I am not a "religious" person, per
se, but I do believe in God and spirituality. The life that
goes unreflected upon, to me, is one that is left empty,
unsuccessful (however that is defined), or without
purpose. Every being has a purpose. Sometimes taking
a deep breath and stopping just for a moment to listen
to that inner voice is all we need to ensure that we are
making a decision that keeps us on our own life path.
That consciousness has importance in everything we
do—what we do for a living, the person we marry, and
how we handle our finances. I believe these actions are

1

ultimately related. While we all start life at different socioeconomic levels, we have seen here in this great country of ours that it can be one's decisions that define how happy and fulfilled of a life we live.

The last year was a tough one for our country and our economy. On the one hand we have seen the triumph of our nation by electing our first African-American president. Regardless of party affiliation, it is clear that Barack Obama is a man who listened to his inner voice and followed his life path. On the other end of the spectrum, however, we have suffered enormous financial losses as a nation and as individuals. The actions of a subset in the population caused us all financial suffering. That subset consists of people who bought a bigger house than they could afford, and those who financed this delivery of an undeserved, premature American dream. This is an example of how the decisions of a few affected the life paths of us all.

I have always tried to listen to my inner voice. Some would call it instinct; others may define it as a nutcase hearing voices inside her head. Up until this point, I would say my life has been anything but boring, and I firmly believe that is because I have always stopped and listened to my gut. This is not to say that I have not made mistakes along the way—no one can honestly make that claim. But what I can say is that when I have made mistakes, it has been as a result of not truly listening to my inner voice.

I have an M.B.A. in finance, but before I earned that degree, I spent a brief amount of time on a path that was not for me. I went through an entire year of law school, learning more contract law than 99 percent of the population, which has served me well in the business world. I dropped out when I had a light-bulb moment and admitted to myself that I was always more interested in investing in the stock market. Fortunately I had very supportive parents who always told me I could achieve whatever I set my mind to. Once I got honest with myself, I knew entering the world of investments was my true path.

During my M.B.A. program, I had the opportunity to explore the various career paths in the investment industry. I had been interested in stock picking since I was 12 years old when my mother let me buy my first share of bank stock after showing an interest in it. So after learning more, I decided to become a portfolio manager since my interest in stock picking could be used best by getting on that career track. But no one just hands over a multimillion-dollar portfolio to a newbie to start managing. In the typical path, step one is to start as an equity analyst. I became an equity analyst, focusing on the bank sector at a small fledgling mutual fund company in the hills of Lancaster, Pennsylvania. This was the mid-1990s, and as I recall, the market was pretty rocky. I remember a couple of scary days when trading curbs were put into effect, and the market was even shut down. It was a baptism by fire for me. Not only was I thrust into analyzing an industry I knew very little about, I had to write research reports on companies and recommend the stocks. That was something I took very seriously. All I could think about was some little old lady reading one of my reports and recommendations before putting her life savings in that stock. What if I was wrong? What if I caused her to lose everything? So I made it my business to thoroughly comprehend the banking sector before I started recommending stocks. I did this by conducting many face-to-face interviews with CEOs and CFOs of banks around the country. I asked about the industry, their institution, and about competition. Within a matter of months, I understood the lay of the land pretty well. I could analyze not only an entire sector, but a company and a management team, too. It is this depth of understanding that has allowed me to be a successful stock picker and investor.

For years I have been tossing around the idea of writing a book, but between managing my business and clients' investments, becoming an author has always taken a backseat. Then 2008 happened—October 9, 2008, to be exact. It was the day the market crashed— CRASHED! It was on that day that I realized all the "truths" that I lived by when it came to investments were not necessarily going to be true in the future. My colleagues and I were shell-shocked for days. I spent hours glued to the television, listening to economists, analysts, reporters, and those who call themselves "personal finance experts." All of the "advice" they were spewing made me realize that if not for my education, training, and experience, I would have been terrified and confused about what to do with my investments. I began to appreciate my experiences even more; hopefully, I can impart my knowledge to help you become a better investor and financial decision maker.

One morning while I was watching the local news in my hometown of Miami, Florida, and I saw a story about a woman and her five-year-old daughter. The two were living in a motel room because they could no longer afford their rental apartment. The mother, very well spoken and intelligent, worked for an insurance operation for several years until she was laid off early in 2009. Despite her best efforts to find another job, she was unsuccessful. They lived day to day. The little girl was adorable, but there was pain and sadness in her eyes. I saw too many stories like this, and I wanted to help. I contacted the television station, and asked them for the woman's e-mail address. Once they provided it for me, I reached out to her. She was happy to talk to me—according to her, the only other contacts she had were men with less than desirable intentions. That made me sad.

After a brief e-mail exchange, she realized I was sincere. She provided me with her phone number. I called her and asked her how much money she had left for the hotel room. She had only enough for one more night. She claimed that they had tried to go to a shelter, but her daughter's asthma became active because of her allergies. I offered to pay for her room at the motel until I could help them find permanent living arrangements. I did not ask questions about her past, her family, or if she had someone to call for help. I surmised if she had family or someone in her life to call, she would have done that already rather than end up homeless. I advised her to immediately find a real estate agent to assist her.

The next 10 days or so were very educational me. I realized that when one becomes "homeless"—which is probably not something many of us stop to think about—an identity is totally lost, and reentering "mainstream" society becomes virtually impossible without a sponsor. How can you look for a job without a computer? I suppose going to the library is a possibility—but with a small child it is difficult to stay long enough to do a proper job search on the Internet. How can you send out a resume when you don't even have an address to put on the heading? I recall one day soon after sending her a bit of cash, my new friend, Jane, smartly went and rented a laptop to continue her job search and stay connected to the world. Until then she had used the public computer at the motel where they were living. That was a great idea—except finding a truly "free" WiFi connection proved very difficult, and it cost her nearly six hours of a day once. Simple things the rest of us take for granted aren't as accessible for the less fortunate; it became clear to me how poverty is a downward spiral that can become virtually impossible to escape—and therefore, all the more reason to make the right decisions to never end up in that position.

On so many levels, poverty becomes debilitating. It makes a person feel like a failure or a criminal—like the person did something wrong. Jane was so afraid to contact a real estate agent to help her find a new place to live because he or she would see Jane's bad credit. I talked her into it by telling her that half the world probably has bad credit, and that we would not stop until we found her a place. Over the next few weeks, she became more comfortable with my help. I could tell she was building back her confidence and self-esteem.

As I wrote this book, I learned that awareness of one's life path is important. Though I hope I can help, I do not think striking it rich is the most important thing when it comes to investing. What is important is living a good life while saving money for a rainy day and, at the same time, being able to enjoy life and family. The truth is, unless you're born with a silver spoon in your mouth, any one of us can end up like my new friend Jane and her daughter if we do not plan. No one should have to go through that. With some "new" common-sense approaches to certain elements of investing and finance, as opposed to some of the "old economy," stale advice being handed out by personal finance gurus, it is possible to avoid that worst-case scenario and live a fulfilled life.

For those unfamiliar with Alan Greenspan, let me explain for a moment who he is and why he's important. Alan Greenspan was the chairman of the Federal Reserve from 1987 to 2006. President Bush nominated Ben Bernanke to assume Mr. Greenspan's role after he served an unprecedented five terms in the position. Mr. Greenspan is often thought of as one of the strongest supporters of laissez-faire capitalism (translation: let the chips fall where they may when something goes wrong with the economy). After the financial meltdown started and was at its peak in September 2008, Mr. Greenspan went before a congressional hearing on October 23, 2008 and declared that his free-market ideology was an incorrect view of the world. This was eye-opening to hear for those of us who over the years had thought Mr.

Greenspan's approach, belief system, and Fed policies had kept the U.S. economy on a fairly even keel. To hear his admittance, in the midst of a stock market crash, was really terrifying to me.

My mission with this book is to save readers the pain and heartache of listening to the same outdated, "old economy," pre-2008 concepts, or *myths*, as I like to call them—especially since even Alan Greenspan admitted he was wrong! This is not to suggest that all of the financial advice out there is incorrect or poor information—some of it is very good. Yes, it is important for everyone to eliminate credit card debt and build up a "rainy day" savings account of six to eight months worth of living expenses. Others have written about those topics, so I see no reason to repeat them. Don't expect a chart in this book to help you figure out your monthly budget. However, when it comes to investment and important financial life concepts, some of the top-selling advice books out there fall short, in my opinion, because they have not adapted to the new world or even tackled topics related to money and investing that most of us now realize we need to actively pay attention to. If you have read some of those other advice books out there, I ask that you try to separate the wheat from the chaff when it comes to investments and banking. My hope is that readers will have a better understanding of how investments and general banking work, and be able to use this knowledge to find their financial life path to long-term prosperity. *Don't Buy the Bull* takes complex concepts and simplifies them, so that everyone can learn something and apply it to their everyday financial life.

CHAPTER 1
THE BIG PICTURE

I find it so interesting that since the market has dropped thousands of points, many of the financial experts out there are backing off and giving little advice about investments. Now is not the time to be shy! If you were, then you probably missed some good opportunities to make some money back. Now is the time when people can utilize what investment dollars they have left to try to create wealth. I think the most important thing is to continue to do those gut checks—only you know whether or not you can actually afford to put more into investments right now, or if you really do need to continue building up that cash cushion. With that said, I hear things that make me cringe on an almost daily basis. It is important to take in all the information and think for yourself; if you listen to some of these myths, what is that going to do to your future? What about the future of your spouse or children?

One of the easiest ways to make sure one gets onto the right financial life path is to start contributing to a retirement plan immediately. Put down this book right now and go find out what type of retirement plan your employer offers and sign up for it at once if you aren't participating already. If you want financial success, contribute money into a retirement account that you cannot touch (with the exception of extreme emergencies). Consistent contributions really will help achieve long-term retirement goals.

When I started out with my first job in the investment business, I remember getting some very sound advice from one of the old-time stockbrokers at the firm. He told me to save into my 401(K) plan until it hurt, and that every time I got a raise I should keep doing that. So I listened to him, and my little 401(K) grew very nicely within a couple of years. In the case of an emergency, I can potentially use this money (although getting access to it may mean paying some penalty fees). When I spoke to Jane, one of the first things I noticed was that she was well educated and employed for many years. Yet, she never contributed to any of the retirement plans that her employers offered, and she therefore deprived herself of money that she could have accessed for hardship. To me, it is never too late to get on the right track. You will surely smile at the end of the year when you see that you have forced yourself to save.

Jane is not yet able to invest, but she will once she is more firmly back on her own feet. And even now when I talk to her, I am surprised by some of her questions related to the subject. She treats the subject of finance as something of which to be afraid and overwhelmed. As a result, she still has difficulty making ends meet even with the financial aid she's received. If she is willing to make a change in how she views money and can get past being intimidated by it, she'll be able to make great strides to have a more positive financial future. I guess that's the lesson here—those who do not get intimidated will probably end up on the right financial life path. Those who continue to be unnerved and scared will most likely end up not having their money work for them because they will continue to ignore the necessary act of gaining knowledge of how to use it properly.

I have put together a number of "myths" that I think need to be addressed immediately, while we are still in the midst of opportunity. By debunking them now, I believe people still have a chance to make the right decisions.

Myth #1

We are in for a long, slow recovery and it will be another five years before the economy is healthy.

Let me remind you of a fact that many of us have forgotten in the last couple of years: we live in the greatest country in the world. I'm not just saying that because I'm a proud American—I'm saying that because I have traveled abroad, and despite some of the positives that our European brethren may have over us in the areas of culture and sophistication, the fact is, our political and economic systems are the best models in the world. I say that now, despite everything, because it is the truth. Even an article in *The Economist* magazine supports my viewpoint—that if given the choice, most adults would choose to live in the United States, with Britain, Canada, or France in close second. Our population would actually expand by 160 million more people if borders were truly open.

Why? We are stable, and the world looks up to our way of life and political system. Our accounting standards are trusted and solid. Our government and political system is considered the most stable, and our workers are considered the most productive in the world. We are truly free and able to make our own decisions for ourselves. Just like Alan Greenspan taught us for years, regulation is bad, right? Take a trip to Canada or the U.K. for a brief time and observe that even in those societies, government has a bit more involvement in daily life, simply because of the heightened level of regulations in their society. I am certainly not saying all regulation is bad—heck, Canada's banking system weathered the last couple of years very successfully. The reason is that there are only a handful of banks in Canada because of regulations on that system. But I think Americans will probably never allow this level of regulation into our free-market system—for many it would be considered a step in the wrong direction. Just look at the "tea parties" popping up all over the country to protest against government getting bigger.

All of these concepts mean our system has substantial integrity and that is really the premise behind this book. My opinion is that our society has created a pathway for those willing to work hard; even for those with very little money or education, success is possible. Surely that must be why so many millions of people want to move to the United States every year. I don't see places like Zimbabwe or Venezuela popping up on *The Economist's* list!

Since the 1850s there have been 32 **business cycles** in the U.S. In almost all cases, job losses continued even after the economy was back on the upswing. So here we are after the 2008 stock market crash with an alarming unemployment rate that politicians believe will still continue to increase beyond the 10 percent level. Most economists will say that this recession is most similar to that of 1981–1982 because that too was a deep recession that lasted 16 months. During that time, unemployment peaked at almost 11 percent. But in that case, the recession was caused, by most accounts, by high interest rates that were used in order to tame inflation—which can be a real economy killer. So for that reason, the recession in the early '70s, in my opinion, seems to parallel a bit more to our current recession. It was, of course, driven by high oil prices, which caused a lack of spending by consumers in the economy and led to an unemployment rate of 9 percent. That recession, as well, lasted 16 months.

A **business cycle** is the period of growth or contraction in the economy.

We have "officially" been in a recession since December 2007, and the rest of the world followed suit sometime in the summer of 2008. Many personal financial gurus told us initially to hunker down because this bad recession was going to last for years and years. But I believe that the concept of a recession lasting years and years is simply not possible, and I don't want readers to walk around terrified every time a normal ebb and flow of the business cycle occurs! When Jane talks about the negative news she hears about the economy, I remind her that most talking heads are just that—not a lot of substance. Logic will prevail so that the outcome for our economy will be positive and follow other historically valid trends.

Not too long ago, our Federal Reserve issued a statement saying it now believes the economy has taken a turn for the better, though it's a small turn. Statistics such as **GDP** growth are offered as proof of a rebound, just as in every other recession. They also continue to caution us that when the economy does start to grow again, it will not do so at a high expansion rate. This is a very important fact, because underlying the stock market has to be an assumption on growth of companies' profits. If the assumptions include low growth, that means lower profit growth—and that in turn could mean it will take longer for the U.S. Dow Jones Industrial Average to regain its 14,000-point high for some time.

GDP (Gross Domestic Product) is the market value of all goods and services produced in the U.S.

I have to say one of the most disturbing parts of this *particular* downturn in the economy has been the lack of hope and leadership coming out of our politicians. The reality is that every politician is saying the same thing—things are bad. Yes, we all know that. However, I think there is an unspoken sentiment attached to the bad news: "But we're working every day to find solutions and help businesses create opportunity and get the credit markets flowing again. We want you to go about your day—working, spending time with family, and trying to enjoy life." Maybe I sound a little basic when I say this, but U.S. consumers are the greatest consumers in the world. We are the engines of growth that drive the rest of the world. While China has created some internal consumer demand over the last decade, most of their products are sold primarily in the U.S. and Europe. With the market crash and the downturn in the economy, we have pulled back our spending, and as a result other countries around the world are earning less. Our recession has driven them into an economic downturn, which means that we need some good old-fashioned consumer confidence. I believe that feeling of confidence starts at the top. Our leaders should set the tone so that the average person knows it is not necessary to walk around so uptight. We need this in every recession. Even going back to the Great Depression, we had leadership that created a "can do" atmosphere from what historical accounts tell us.

I believe that with our new president, Barack Obama, and his administration, this is happening because many view him as such an inspirational figure. I also believe that by fixing the capital adequacy issues of the banks, the stock market has been greatly stabilized. Remember, what drove us to a Great Depression in the 1930s was the collapse of our banking system. At the time the Federal Reserve did not act quickly enough to boost liquidity in the banking system by pumping in more dollars. This time around, we were able to avoid a complete global financial meltdown (and therefore another Great Depression) because our Federal Reserve acted quickly and realized that the way to get control of the crisis was to help the banks, not let them fail. As that aid was given to the banks, the stock market started to stabilize in the spring of 2009. If we ever have another crisis again, pay attention to how quickly the Federal Reserve springs into action. This will be a good guidepost as to how markets will react. I think a good rule of thumb is this: a quick reaction should lead to a quicker bounce back in the market, at least initially.

All this is intertwined with the concept of consumer confidence. A major psychological factor is associated with the rise of the market. Confidence will be restored. As consumers feel safe again, they will start to spend more. Without this psychological factor, our economy simply won't be able to move forward. Make no mistake, I don't think people should spend money needlessly or drive up their credit card bills, but it is important for everyone to realize that their actions, no matter how small, will help our economy. I know this may be a hard concept for some readers to grasp, but everything in our economy is intertwined. One layoff at a manufacturing plant affects not only the unemployed worker, but many companies, the people who touch the life of that worker, and the manufacturing plant at which he or she worked. So, this is why even the smallest increase in consumer spending can start to reverse a contracting economy and job losses.

According to several economic studies, the stock market generally bottoms out when the economy is at its weakest. Historically, the most pessimistic time for the economy actually created the best time to buy stocks. Generally speaking, the stock market starts to turn up, even after the economy is still in recession. Since the '50s there have been nine recessions, and the stock market has primarily reacted the same way. In each case, the market gains ranged from 18 percent to 58 percent within six months of the economic low with a mean of 36 percent. *This recession has been no different,* despite the scary swings we witnessed and the brink of disaster our economy faced. As I write this, we are up over 50 percent off the lows the stock market hit in March 2009. This is why it is important to know a bit about history. Next time, maybe you can be prepared to watch for those lows and consider it an entry point into the market for some great returns as the stock market pulls itself back up!

Myth #2
Now is the time to buy low and hold for 10, 15, 20 years or more.

As I've stated, the world has changed, and the rules of the investing game have changed. Being a defensive investor is just as important as being a defensive driver; under no circumstance should you ever buy a stock with the intent of holding it for 10, 15, 20 years or more. I have heard this advice many times in the last several months, and it has to be the most dangerous advice in my opinion. My heart breaks when I hear voices of the new generation refusing to sell inherited stocks for "sentimental" reasons, or when a family member is unwilling to **diversify** a large stock position to more evenly distribute risk because it pays a good **dividend**. Here are just a few real life examples of stocks like this:

- Wachovia Bank – This stock traded at $37.17 per share on January 2, 2008. The company was recently sold to Wells Fargo in a forced sale for less than $7 per share.

- Lehman Brothers – This stock traded at more than $60 per share in early 2008. The company is now bankrupt. The stock is now worth about $0.10 per share.

- General Motors – This stock traded at $24.41 per share on January 2, 2008. Since then, of course, the government had to intervene. The company declared bankruptcy in early 2009 and emerged from bankruptcy protection. The stock recently traded at only $0.61 per share under a liquidation stock symbol.

To **diversify** simply means holding a variety of investments and asset classes (i.e., stocks and bonds) so that if one part of a portfolio underperforms, the rest of the portfolio will hopefully do well in order to keep the portfolio stable or growing.

A **dividend** is a payment of a portion of corporate profits paid to shareholders of that corporation.

If you cannot spend adequate time, or you are uncomfortable with investments, then I strongly recommend hiring a professional money manager to oversee your financial endeavors. You could also use **ETFs** to diversify your investments in stocks and do minimal work. However, watching the investments on a daily or weekly basis *will still be important*. Remember, the key to all investment and financial decisions is that you are at the center of them. *Hiring a professional does not mean you should take your eyes off your money.*

An **ETF** is an Exchange-Traded Fund. These are baskets of holdings, similar to a mutual fund. But they trade in real time just like a share of stock, typically have lower fees than a mutual fund, and have transparency of what is held inside the fund.

This book is not intended to teach readers about how to pick stocks. However, I am going to give a few basic tips to help you understand the importance of reexamining stock positions and to determine whether an ownership position in the company remains a good idea or if it is time to sell. There were warning signs with the aforementioned companies that were indicative of danger. Let's start with change. Whenever there is an important change at a company, a decision to buy or hold should be made. The types of change must be examined, and all of these announcements can be found either by looking at the company's investor relations website and signing up for automatic updates when news comes out. Or check a financial website such as Yahoo Finance every day:

- Senior management changes: CEO retired or is fired, changes in other key spots all at the same time and/or board changes.

- Management and/or board is selling stock.

- Dividends are being cut.

- The company's product or service is either be- coming obsolete or losing market share.

- The company's product or service is becoming a commodity, and it is losing pricing power.

- The company is no longer in the first or second market position in the industry.

- Continuous negative earnings surprises—the company misses analysts' earnings estimates.

The bullets above have the same thing in com- mon—they have to do with a *fundamental* change in the company or its business model that is brought about for various reasons. For example, if the CEO is a longstanding, respected part of the company, then his or her retirement will not come as a surprise most likely. But if he or she has been a controversial pick, and the "retirement" is so abrupt that a search must take place while an "interim" CEO holds the posi- tion, then that is a signal that the company might be in for a rough patch. Some of the companies I men- tioned earlier are examples of this—both GM and

Wachovia Bank had senior management changes in abrupt manners.

In the case of insider stock ownership, I think it is an important vote of confidence to see insiders buying stock. It shows they believe in the company's future success and market position going forward. But when management sells stock, it is a strong signal that any investor in that company should follow suit. According to Securities and Exchange's Angelo Mozzilo—then CEO of Countrywide Financial—sold $129 million in stock, according to Securities and Exchange filings, the year before the collapse of Countrywide for "diversification reasons." As I see it, however, he got out when he saw the top of the mortgage industry—and this should have been a clear signal of trouble for other owners of that stock that it was probably time for them to sell, too.

Sometimes good companies just have stocks that get ahead of themselves. Often you'll see when a stock runs up quickly, management will sell some of their holdings. That means they believe it's overpriced, and they're taking advantage of the run-up. That means you should, too! Because you sell at that moment does not mean you are never going to own the stock again, it just means that you sold the stock for a high price, then waited for the value to increase. When the time is right, you can buy it again.

The point I am trying to make is that the old-world myth of buy and hold for a long, long time—no matter how great of a company we are talking about—is just a bad idea. Technology advances too quickly; it is impossible to say today's high-flying tech company will be tomorrow's superstar. This concept applies to every industry; it requires investment practicality—having the ability to say it's time to take my profits and go, or it's time to cut my losses early rather than wait for a potential turnaround. While I cannot say that in every case you may not leave a little profit on the table, I would like to remind readers of an Irish proverb: *Bulls get rich, bears get rich, but pigs get slaughtered.*

Myth #3
The problem with being out of the market is that when it turns around, you will never make up for your losses if you miss the rallies.

Market timing is very difficult. Many investors believe it is important to be in the market in time to take advantage of the next big rally because a good percentage of overall return might come from the initial leg up in a "bull market"—an upswing in the market. While that may be the case, I believe it is important for people to sleep at night. If you were invested in the market prior to the market crash, then you may not have pulled money out of the market before things got really ugly. As a result, you may have suffered through quite a bit of volatility and pain that caused quite a number of sleepless nights. Only you know yourself. If you are the type of person that gets very upset and nervous every time the market turns negative, it means you probably need to wait for the market to have a bit of momentum behind it before you get in. That may mean the next time this happens, as long you are paying attention, you have the opportunity to sell out of the market and sit in cash for a while. Yes, you will miss out on a very important leg up in a market rally and miss a "home run," but you'll also save yourself a lot of physical and mental turmoil. You will still do well; it just means hitting more singles and doubles to get there.

It is important to remember that there are no set answers, only shades of gray when it comes to the decision of when to invest. Knowing oneself is a big part of determining how much and when to invest. Yes, the old adage of "buy low, sell high" certainly should apply—but the questions to ask are: "How will I feel if I buy low, and the stock goes lower? How will I be able to handle that emotionally?" If the answer is that your stomach will churn, perhaps this strategy of always being invested in the market does not work for you.

I also want to say that I believe it is an important part of any investment portfolio strategy to have cash on the sidelines in case a good quality investment happens to trade down for no fundamental reason. I know some "experts" will disagree with me on this, but those who had 95 percent of their money in the market in the fall of 2008 will tell you they probably wished they had moved into cash more quickly at that time. If in fact you are always fully invested, you'll never be able to take advantage of short-term opportunities when they come along. But again, in a market downturn, don't expect or try to buy at the very bottom. If you do buy on a downturn, don't be surprised if the market (and therefore the stock you just purchased) turns down a bit further before going back up. Just think of a rollercoaster—if you are anything like me, then you will hope for a smooth ride on a Ferris wheel but expect the Six Flags triple loop!

Myth #4
The best thing to do is to stay invested, stay the course.

We often hear the phrase "stay the course" when it comes to investing strategy. As the market was crashing, I'd hear expert after expert give that same piece of advice. Basically what it means is just doing more of the same—keeping your investments right where they are and riding out a downturn. There is so much wrong with this concept of "stay invested, stay the course." What exactly would make anyone want to stay fully invested right now or ever again for that matter? Do we have any assurances that the market won't ever retest the March 2009 bottom ever again? What if it happens a few more times? If we all stayed put with our investments, no one would be able to take advantage of low stock prices created by a downturn. In talking to lay people about this concept of buy low, sell high, I hear the recurring theme about brokers trying to convince people to stay fully invested. I do not know their intentions behind this advice, but do not listen to them. Selling stock gives you the buying power to purchase low. If you have no liquid funds to buy on dips when you encounter a downturn in your lifetime, for whatever the reason or whenever it happens, remember to run for the exit sign first in order to sit on your cash pile. Those out of the market first will be there to watch it fall, preparing to utilize their funds sitting on the sidelines when they are ready to invest again.

Staying the course also implies that the same stocks will work in any environment—or for that matter, the same sector ETF or mutual fund. The world can change—in a positive or negative way—in relatively short order. Look how quickly oil traded down from $146 a barrel down to the mid-30s just months later. Can you imagine if you "stayed the course" and kept your investment in an oil-related stock or fund?

Again, it goes back to being aware of what's going on out there. If you can't devote the time to this, then get some professional help. If you prefer not to get help from an advisor, then consider becoming so diversified in your investment that it will not matter. While that level of diversification and "autopilot" investments will lead to returns that might not be as strong, you may be more comfortable with being a do-it-yourselfer. Whichever way you choose to invest, just remember that it's your money and your future. No matter what kind of account you have—a brokerage account or 401(K), I urge you to take it all seriously—don't discount your investments or devote less attention to them just because they are in a 401(K). And even if your 401(K) plan at work has only very basic investment options, you still need to watch those investments like you would any others. That means enter the symbols into Yahoo Finance, Bing, or any other financial home page of your choice, and follow these stocks every day. Or, if you're old fashioned, pull out the business section of the newspaper and follow them in the stock quote pages. If you see the market is turning negative, then consider putting your money in the cash equivalent of the 401(K) plan investment feature for a little while (a few days, a week, even a month, or even longer). Do this when you think the market is getting a bit shaky. Then take the time to see what has shifted in the economy, the market, and the world to see if the investment selections you had previously are still appropriate. Chances are, you will determine it's time to make some new selections and take advantage of different opportunities. It is the act of being proactive and taking control that will help keep you on a successful financial life path.

CHAPTER 2
INVESTING FOR INCOME

O ver the last year I have heard people of all net worths tell me they are scared to death of the stock market. I believe many will never get back into the market—whether it is a good idea for them to be out forever and not have the potential for growth is up to them. For those unwilling to take the leap back into the market because their inner voice just won't let them, the natural alternative is at least to put money to use and earn some income from it. But there are some misnomers about how to invest for income—myths that I will abolish right here and now!

Myth #5
Never put tax-free bonds into a tax-deferred investment account.

Recall at the beginning of this book I said that the rules of the game have changed. The type account you place **tax-free bonds** in is an example of this shift. A year ago, I would have agreed with this myth and told readers that tax-free bonds were pointless to put in a tax-deferred investment account because it would not result in being able to take advantage of the tax-free income. Now, all I care about is making money and good investments—tax implications aside.

Examples of **tax-free bonds** include: municipal bonds can be double (state and federal) tax-free and U.S. Treasury securities are federally tax-free.

Only once in a great while are there historic times to invest in municipal bonds. Now is one of those times because municipal bonds currently have attractive prices relative to U.S. Treasury bonds. After-tax yields on a municipal bond may be better than what a U.S. Treasury bond yields. Snapping up high quality municipal bonds and putting them in any type of portfolio is a good idea, and they can be purchased below **par** value because the price of the bond will most likely rise as the market's credit improves. In the past, it made no sense to put them in a tax-advantaged account, but when this phenomenon occurs only so often, it is important to take advantage of these new rules of the game.

Par typically means 100 cents on the dollar.

The credit markets began seizing in the summer of 2007—and this eventually came to light for the average person during the fall of 2008, when Lehman Brothers and AIG Insurance were on the brink of bankruptcy. Credit that was once easily available for local and state municipalities began to dry up. No longer could a municipality issue a new bond in order to pay for an improvement in the municipality, such as a new school, or fund their operations. In addition, most of the major municipal bond insurance companies got into trouble, too. As both of these scenarios started to occur, investors gathered cash and sold municipal bonds. The result—the actual prices of the bonds fell. In many cases, good quality, high investment grade municipal bonds traded down to **70 or 80 cents on the dollar.** That means, in addition to collecting the coupon (interest, usually expressed as a percentage) payment from the bond, an investor had the potential of earning a healthy cash return on the bond itself as investor confidence returned. This additional return was, of course, on top of collecting the coupon payment from the bond. My rationale is simple. Those bonds should trade back to par or higher as our credit markets normalize and emotions come back to earth. Most municipal bonds have traded back to higher prices again, depending on credit rating, geography, and type of municipal bond.

MUNICIPAL BONDS IN 2007

Bond par = 100 cents on the dollar
Coupon = 5 percent
# of years to maturity = 4
Tax-equivalent yield = 5 percent divided by (1 minus your tax rate, say 25 percent) = 6.66 percent

---

MUNICIPAL BONDS IN 2010

Same bond, but priced at 80 cents on the dollar
Coupon = 5 percent
# of years to maturity = 4
Current yield = 5 percent divided by 80 = 6.25 percent
Tax-equivalent yield = same as 2007

Just as is the case with stocks, keep in mind that there can be a difference in the quality of municipal bonds because of the difference in quality of a particular state's attributes. For example, California was on front-page media almost daily in 2008 because of its cash flow issues (the state even issued IOUs to creditors). That was caused by the fact that their tax revenues were not enough to support the governmental infrastructure of the state—i.e., pay state employees, run important social services, and, of course, pay the interest on the state's municipal bonds. When a state's revenues are in question like this, there is speculation that the state will not be able to pay for their obligations and service their debt, so expect their municipal bond issues to trade down to low prices. The flip side of this would be a state such as South Dakota, which has a relatively stable revenue base due to low unemployment. In that circumstance, do not expect a quality state municipal bond to trade down to the same low levels. However, in a broad market de-cline (like the one we witnessed in the fourth quarter of 2008), when the only thing happening is large investors running for the exit signs and throwing the proverbial baby out with the bathwater, it may be possible to buy a quality state municipal bond opportunistically, at a level that does not happen very often. This means the dollar price of the municipal bond will hopefully rise, if all goes according to plan. So, in addition to earning the 3 per-cent or 4 percent tax-free interest payment on the bond, an investor may be able to gain an extra 5 to 30 percent upside on the underlying price of the municipal bond. In fact, paying attention resulted in great returns on bonds in recent history for this reason.

While I have no crystal ball, the investment scenario I am laying out is most commonly observed when there are ebbs and flows with every kind of bond—municipal bonds or otherwise. Being aware of when the tide is in your favor is the mark of someone staying true to his or her financial life plan. The fact is that credit and stock markets go in cycles; as they continue to improve, the Federal Reserve keeps interest rates low until it's clear that we are on a path out of recession. As that happens, the higher yields will become harder to find without risk. Why? Think back to periods when interest rates were very low—try finding a savings account that pays a good rate or a one-year CD paying even 2 percent!

At certain times in the economy when the federal government is trying to stimulate growth, it wants businesses to invest in growth, so it keeps interest rates low. For the average investor that means earning interest on cash cannot happen in a regular savings account. So the first places investors will need to look is at high quality corporate and municipal bonds. This divergence from normal bond pricing can occur in various sectors of the bond market during abnormal credit cycles, so keep your eyes open. The next time, there might be opportunities only in the corporate bond sector rather than the municipal bonds or treasuries. Therefore, odd times call for being opportunistic and using innovative strategies—go ahead and buy those municipal bonds and put them in any portfolio you need to (IRA account or taxable account) in order to make some money!

Myth #6
Invest in individual stocks with high dividends to generate income.

There have been countless times when a client has said to me, "How about putting money into high dividend-paying stocks?" That high dividend-paying stocks are always a good investment is one of the oldest myths. If only it were that easy. But in life, there's always a catch. Under the right circumstances, putting money into one of these stocks can be a really good idea. Why? The concept behind this myth, some theorize, is basically that even if the stock never moves, the investor is earning something equivalent to or better than what they would get in a bank account or a shorter term bank CD. In a good scenario, for example, if I bought 100 shares of XYZ stock at $10 each and was paid $0.35 per share each year, that would be a 3.5 percent dividend yield. That may be a great yield in comparison to what I can make in a CD. I may think that XYZ company is boring with not a lot of growth potential, but not a lot of downside risk either. So, even if the stock sits at $10 for a couple of years, I'm collecting my dividend for income or for reinvestment purposes. This scenario requires knowing that XYZ is a rock solid company with a stable management and balance sheet. The bottom line is that to practice this, you have to operate under the principle that the dividend is *safe*. It also assumes that the company is so predictable, it does not have a lot of earnings growth, which is why the stock may not be one that will move a lot.

Despite this neat little theory, according to the Schwab Center for Financial Research, historically, dividend-yielding stocks have underperformed on a total return basis. Keep in mind that total return on a stock is not just how much the stock price appreciates, but the amount of dividend yield collected on the stock. From 1990 to 2008, this research group found the average 12-month total returns on dividend-paying stocks was 15.7 percent as opposed to 18 percent on non-dividend-paying stocks.

Unfortunately, what we have witnessed in recent history is that some of those "safe" stocks that paid solid dividends (including some of our most well-known companies, like financial institutions and insurance companies) ended up having major issues in this last recession, and those unwavering dividends either vanished completely or got chopped in half or more. It is not written in stone that a company must pay a dividend. And it is not a guarantee that once a company starts paying a dividend it must continue to pay a consistent dividend, or even pay one at all from year to year.

Examples of well-known stocks that have cut or eliminated dividends in recent history:

- Pfizer
- Bank of America
- Citigroup
- General Electric

- Dow Chemical
- CBS Corporation
- *The New York Times*

*Source: *The Wall Street Journal*

I'll hear someone say, "That stock is paying a 7, 8, or even 9 percent dividend yield. I'll buy some of that. I can afford to wait for the stock to go up, and I could use the extra income." I'll let you in on a secret that smart money managers have known for years: what that actually means is that the stock price is already down, ahead of the presumption that the dividend will be altered in some negative way. The "smart money," otherwise known as Wall Street, hedge funds, and mutual funds, have already moved out of the stock because they figured out the dividend is going to be cut or may even go away. That is why the stock is down (and the yield is up). As soon as that dividend is cut, the stock will look like just an average stock paying a 3 or 4 percent dividend, or maybe no dividend, depending on the situation. For example, if we took our same XYZ stock from the previous example, now trading at $5 per share, the dividend yield is now at 7 percent, paying the same $0.35 per share, that stock looks attractive. However, this is a big red flag. Most likely the story will end with this company announcing to the world that it is having some difficulties, and needs to keep its cash inside the company rather than pay out to shareholders for a while. The stock most likely will not react at this point—it's already dropped to $5 per share, after all, and the dividend yield will change to zero since the company stated it will pay no dividend for a while. So much for that great buy and hold strategy of owning a high dividend-yielding stock.

There are a few more points I want to make in order to clarify my view on this myth. First, not all dividend-yielding stocks are created equally. There are many of them that have very safe dividend payments and, therefore, are worth owning. In some situations they can be a solid investment that is worth it when the dividend payments are reinvested. But before buying one of these stocks, some real homework is needed. Don't just listen to what someone tells you—part of sticking to your financial life path is being conscious of your finances for yourself—and that includes your investments. So unless you plan on hiring an investment professional, doing some research for yourself becomes important. The best way to do this is to look at the company's own investor relations website—which every public company has. Somewhere on that site will be a place that shows you the levels of **dividend payout ratios** the company maintained in the past. This ratio will give you an idea of how well the company's income can support the dividend it is paying out to shareholders. The key is consistency—the more consistent and the longer the track record, the better it is. However, as we saw in the last year or so, this is a perfect example of how "past performance does not guarantee future results." So what that means is that even once you identify what appears to be a solid company with a consistent dividend, there is still no guarantee the dividend is entirely safe.

Dividend payout ratio is the annual dividend per share divided by earnings per share.

The next step in your process is to look at the big picture. Is this a stock in an industry that is having some problems? Using recent history as an example, pretty much everyone knew there were issues in the banking system (Citigroup, Wachovia, Washington Mutual, Bank of America, just to name a few), and manufacturing companies with finance arms (GM and General Electric). So, if you had identified what initially appeared to be a few solid dividend-paying stocks, then realized that they were in an industry having some problems, that is an indication that you still have some work to do to find a company with a solid dividend.

Generally, professional investors look to certain consumer staple stocks for solid dividends. Let this be your guidepost, too. These are the types of companies that may not grow their top line revenues by very much, maybe only 1 or 2 percent a year, but they make necessities, such as toilet paper or soap. In fact, when these types of stocks start to perform better, it is a sure sign that we're headed for a downturn. Why? Because when a downturn seems imminent, investors look to safe haven stocks with consistent revenues. This is something everyone can follow for him or herself, though it takes constant awareness, since it means having to be aware of the time when it is ready to put money to work. The moment to buy in might be when the economy has been humming along for a while and all of a sudden you realize there may be some signs the economy may be slowing down. Or that moment may be visible and stomach churning, such as the one we had in October 2008. The market plummeted by thousands of points and huge dips in the stocks of many of the world's best companies made it look like their dividends were too good to be true. It is in these moments, if you've already done your homework and you're at the right place at the right time to help your financial life path, to buy some of that dividend stock you may have been following for a while. It is important to identify the stocks you want, and wait for the right time to buy them. Otherwise, you may risk underperformance.

I have one final note about investing in high dividend-yielding stocks. This applies specifically to older folks or those who say they need more income out of their investments. If you fall into one of those two camps, please do not buy a stock in order to provide you with income—use bonds. Generally speaking, stocks are more volatile and the money you invest in a stock may be worth more or less every single day. Sure, a stock might pay a good dividend and you might collect a nice dividend check every quarter, but your principle may be going up and down like a rollercoaster. If you want to introduce a little income generation into your portfolio, or you need to supplement your income, do not look at dividend stocks for this. Use the right tool, which would be bonds.

Myth #7
Always shop around for the highest yielding savings accounts.

My background in analyzing banks for many years has given me a real insight into what makes them tick. For the most part, they all operate by lending money at a higher rate than they pay out on deposits, though some banks approach gathering those deposits differently. This is a really important subtle nuance for consumers to understand in order to have a safe and successful relationship with a bank.

We all think it is a good idea to find the bank paying out the higher yielding savings, however, that can be a dangerous game to play under certain circumstances. In bank lingo, depositors who shop around for a high-paying savings account or CD are called "hot money." A lot of people, particularly retired individuals, who need income, reason that if it is an FDIC-insured deposit and it's a high rate, then it must be a good deal. But anyone using that rationale may not be seeing the forest through the trees. Yes, the FDIC insurance is a good thing. For accounts up to $250,000, there is no question that the FDIC insurance will protect you. If you have more than that, is it a good idea to deposit all of it? Remember, banks thrive on deposits. They need deposits to keep them going. Sometimes when they need deposits, they go out and raise them by making themselves the highest paying rate in the market area. So if you see a bank offering the highest interest rate in your local area—maybe by a little or maybe by a lot— be very suspicious. I always tell friends who ask me if they should put money in a CD that if it is in the middle of the pack of the interest rates, it's okay. But if they tell me it is a CD that is paying a rate at the top of the market, it is probably not that safe. For example, in the fall of 2008, Wachovia Bank was paying the highest rates around the country. Secretly, they were losing deposits as quickly as they were bringing them in, and they were trying to stay afloat. The moral of the story here is, of course, getting paid is always a good thing, but you have to question why a bank is willing to pay top of the market rates when no one else is. You have to ask these questions in order to protect yourself and your money.

If you happen to be one of the fortunate few that have more than $250,000 to keep in the bank, there are a couple of alternatives to consider in order to keep your money safe. The first is to find a bank in your neighborhood that is part of the Certificate of Deposit Account Registry Service (CDARS) program. This program works through participating banks and allows you to deposit up to $50 million in a participating bank and remain FDIC insured. Basically, it works by moving your money into deposit accounts (electronically, of course) at other banks so that you maintain less than the $250,000 limit in any one bank in order to spread out your deposits and remain insured. For more information on this program, visit www.cdars.com.

The other alternative to consider, which may be slightly less expensive because it does not use a middleman, is to work with your financial advisor to buy CDs from solid banks all over the country. Obviously this means only buying CDs under $250,000 to ensure the FDIC insurance is still in force, but the result is the same—spreading the money around to many banks in order to keep all your savings under the limit per institution.

Myth #8

REITs are great because they have such a high dividend and payout ratio.

As I am sure readers have learned by now, one of my general principles is that there is no real black and white when it comes to finance. It all depends on an individual's life situation (job, income, marital status, etc.), as well as timing and opportunity. Investing in **REITs (Real Estate Investment Trusts)** is no different. I am not going to say too much about REITs because we already talked about high dividend-paying stocks (and REITs generally pay high dividends), but I will say that in the past, REITs were viewed as a great investment that gave

investors of all sizes the ability to get involved in real
estate and receive a pay out of 90 percent of income
to shareholders. That means it could have a very high
dividend. This is because of the fact that, by their
nature, REITs were designed to encourage investment in real estate when the structure was created by
the federal government decades ago. In exchange for
this investment in real estate, the government gave
REITs a great tax advantage as long as they paid out
at least 90 percent of net income to shareholders as
dividends. This is a great thing for those of us who
want to be involved in real estate more passively. But
again, that dividend has to be *safe* to make it a good
investment.

An **REIT** owns and/or manages income-
producing properties and must pay out 90
percent of its income to shareholders as
dividends. By paying out that high dividend,
the REIT avoids paying corporate income
tax.

There are so many different types of REITs that
depending on where we are in the economic cycle,
it may or may not be a good time for investing in

a certain type of REIT. REITs traditionally alter their dividend payout ratios more than the average stock. This is because the average office building REIT or mall REIT will have some lumpiness in operations—they may sell a building and realize a one-time gain from that sale, which may result in a larger than average quarterly dividend. The reverse could also occur: when increases in vacancy rates affect rental income numbers, the REIT decreases the amount it pays out.

Types of REITs:
Mortgage REITs
Mall REITs
Apartment REITs
Hotel REITs
Hybrid REITs

I believe REITs can be a great place to invest at the right time in an economic cycle. They offer the average investor a way to invest in real estate without having to do it him or herself, and because a REIT owns many different properties, they provide great diversification. This is a situation where it is important to follow your gut and pay attention to the real estate and economic cycle. When you're buying a house, you know when it's a good deal and when it's not. Think of that on a much bigger scale. Those are the same decisions the professionals who run RE-ITs have to make every day. If you think it's time to buy real estate, then they probably do, too. Those with cash in hand will cut the best deals. Ultimately, those that own the REITs at some point in the future may do well because they will have gotten in after the dust has settled. For a while, investors might be able to collect a solid dividend payment, but these are **cyclical**. It is important to know that investing in REITs is not something you want to do forever; it is great to own real estate directly that you can pay off and keep forever, but with REIT stocks, you must know when to get in and when to get out, using them to your advantage as part of an investment portfolio, and that makes them pay off for you.

A **cyclical stock** moves in the same direction as the economy. For example, when the economy is starting to slow, these stocks usually underperform because the underlying company is tied to the health of the economy.

Myth #9

Safe investments include Treasury notes, CDs, Ginnie Maes, and defined annuities that guarantee an interest rate.

At the top of the list of "safe" investments includes instruments that are backed by the full faith and credit of the United States Government. These are considered ultra safe because non-repayment is virtually impossible. These instruments would include not only U.S. Treasuries, but **Ginnie Mae securities** as well. Generally, anything backed by the U.S. Treasury will not pay as much interest, since there isn't a risk. Other financial investments considered "safe" (as far as return on principal if holding it until maturity) include Certificates of Deposits and insurance annuities. Though getting the principal back is guaranteed, there are certain *pricing* risks in putting money into Treasury notes, CDs, Ginnie Mae securities, or annuities that pay a guaranteed interest because it can lock investors into a permanent interest rate. That can be very dangerous, depending on where certain outside forces are going, such as inflation, economic growth, and outlook for the future.

A **Ginnie Mae security** is a mortgage-backed security that guarantees investors the payment of principal and interest and it is the only MBS security to carry the full faith and credit guarantee of the United States Government.

For those on a fixed income or approaching retirement, the risk is that as inflation becomes more prevalent, any money locked into these "safe investments" will not yield enough to cover the inflation rate, let alone exceed it. The only way the investment can yield enough is if the price of that investment drops; this way, it pays the same yield as a new issue security while the inflation rate is higher. At maturity, the investor is fully repaid. But if the money is needed before maturity, this fixed income investment may or may not be sold at the same price it was purchased—so the entire dollar amount originally invested could be unavailable until maturity date. Keep in mind that in the case of a fixed rate CD, there is always a penalty for early withdrawal.

In the case of an **annuity**, there are different risks than those associated with buying a fixed income investment. The people who sell annuities make a ton of commission income, so I put them into the category of a product that is sold, not bought. In theory, they can be a good idea for people who are in need of a fixed income because they do guarantee a person a set amount from the annuity contract. That certainty can provide a great deal of mental comfort when we see such a volatile stock market. But when interest rates move in the right direction, or the stock market goes up big, the extra gain ends up with the insurance company, depending on the type of annuity. For that reason, younger people that do not need to have a fixed income should not consider investing in an annuity in most circumstances. While it may mitigate downside losses, it greatly limits upside gains, which hurts younger people trying to save for their retirement years. I think keeping investments in a flexible state is most important until really close to retirement. Give yourself as many options as possible. Do you really want to commit to putting money into a set investment like that? I believe in keeping dollars in investments that are as liquid as possible, so that you can access it when you want to, on your own terms. Remember, the name of the game is putting you back in the driver's seat, and flexibility is part of achieving that success.

An **annuity** is a contract entered into with an insurance company, which guarantees a set distribution schedule of payments back to the owner of the contract. That income stream is often on a fixed payment schedule.

There is something else to consider when you think of a "safe investment" and the goal is just to get your money back plus earn a little bit of interest. Remember that it means giving up a potential return on your investment. Ask yourself this question: given where you are in your life, will you kick yourself two years from now when you're locked into a five-year CD at 2 percent with a going rate of 6 percent? Or will you regret buying an investment like a fixed annuity paying maybe only 4 percent if in four years the inflation rate is 6 percent? If the answer is no, then maybe it's a good investment, but if the answer is yes, then this is not the right thing for you to do. For those of us who are not retired, we may find we have needs for our money, such as funding an education, starting a business, etc. and may need access to it. Locking it up in something completely safe may not be the right thing simply because of the lack of access. So have a conversation with yourself (and preferably your financial advisor) before committing to one of these safe but strict investments.

CHAPTER 3
INVESTING FOR GROWTH

Recent history has shown us that a credit crunch and a lack of available credit can stop us in our tracks from borrowing for things like houses, cars, and college educations. I want to assure you that not all banks and bankers are created equally. There are many thousands of banks and bankers out there who know what they are doing, and they lend money every single day. And there always will be lending, whether our economy is growing or in a recession.

Despite the fact that I believe the game has changed for investing because we are in this new economy, I want readers to understand that I support using stocks as part of an investment portfolio under the correct circumstances. Those circumstances are described here in this chapter. As I earlier stated, stocks should never be used as a way to generate income, because of the up and down nature of the stock's price every day. But, if growing your money is more important to you than preserving money, then investing with stocks is going to be an important part of that strategy.

There are many ways to invest for growth. This is where I think it is my job in this book to bust some myths, especially when it comes to how to invest for growth using stocks. At the heart of all these strategies is investing in stocks. But investing in stocks comes in many different "wrappers." Some of those wrappers, I believe, are outdated given some of the newer products that have been created in the last few years. The result is better choices for the average investor, despite how much money you may have to invest.

Myth #10
Mutual funds always make more sense than individual stocks.

I laugh when I hear financial experts talk about investment options; most immediately start talking about mutual funds as some sort of default option we should all put our money into. Apparently, we should all pile into mutual funds because the whole world must consist of idiots who cannot figure out how to buy good quality individual stocks. In my opinion, mutual funds should not be anyone's default option in this day and age. *Don't buy that bull!* First of all, mutual funds can be really expensive. There are expenses built into them such as management fees and marketing fees. Think about it: even in the best year, on January 1st, you will start out in the hole for anywhere from 0.5 percent to as much as 3 percent because of all the fees that are built into the fund. As a person who used to actually give fund managers stock picking ideas, I can tell you that a lot of these fund "managers" don't necessarily make the best or most unique investment decisions. In fact, if you examine the biggest **brand name funds**, you will find that many have the same stocks as their major holdings. These are the names that you and I all know. And all those mutual funds at major firms will probably own the same things in their top holding: Microsoft, Abbott Labs, Coca Cola, and McDonald's; the household brands that you consider solid companies simply because they are big brand names.

Three **brand name fund** examples are AIM, American Century, and Fidelity. Top holdings that overlap include: Microsoft, Abbott Labs, Proctor & Gamble, Johnson & Johnson, and Coca Cola. Good websites to examine mutual funds include Morningstar. com and Smartmoney.com.

You might own five funds or the same stocks five times. For example, I bet virtually every person who owned a large cap mutual fund owned Enron stock years ago, but perhaps they would not have known it because the fund manager dumped it before the end of the quarter. This is because the fund manager **window dressed** the portfolio before quarter-end reporting. To me, that means it is difficult to really know what a fund manager's investment style or philosophy really is. I recommend looking beyond those top holdings and examining the full list of holdings—even the small holdings in the fund should give an insight into what kind of picks that manager is truly investing in. That list may be surprising. There may be actually some stocks that imploded in the quarter on that detailed list, but unless you had actually done the extra homework, you would not have known that. This is why I just don't like mutual funds—there's a lack of transparency. So, unless you're forced into using mutual funds in a 401(K), there are better ways to invest.

Window dressing is the practice that is often used by fund managers to sell loser positions before the quarter's end and replace them with the stocks that were the strongest during the quarter in order to "dress up" the portfolio before the holdings list has to be disclosed to investors in a prospectus. Typically, this is done in the final few days at the end of a quarter.

The case against using mutual funds as the primary way to invest is even more pronounced in a volatile market environment. In addition to lack of transparency with what stocks or securities you own in these funds, there is no ability to execute on a moment's notice. With mutual funds, one huge downside is the necessity to wait until the following day to execute a fund sale. That lack of real-time market inhibits your ability to make your money grow. Selling instantly also gives an investor the opportunity to protect his or her money quickly. In this volatile new world we are living in, the opportunity to move quickly in real time is extremely important. I recall one day during the height of the crisis when the market was still initially dropping, that I literally watched the Dow Jones Industrial Average fall 700 points within only a matter of minutes. While I am sitting at my desk paying attention to this intently in order to protect my clients' money, you may be sitting at your desk doing your work—totally unaware. But even if you were aware of that market drop and you log in to your 401(K) account, none of the changes you want to make to your investments happen instantly—they take a day. That can make things a little painful for a portfolio. But with individual investments or ETFs, trading immediately can hopefully lead to better protection of your hard-earned investment portfolio.

There's one final negative that can catch some investors by complete surprise—and that's a tax bill. Generally, because most mutual funds trade in and out of stocks during the year, they have a "turnover," which in many cases can be more than 100 percent of the fund. That produces gains for the shareholders of the mutual fund. Even if the fund share price ends the year at a lower price than where it started, in many years there can still be a taxable gain to the shareholders because of all the trading done that generated individual gains throughout the year. That can be a big surprise to many investors in mutual funds. Again this leads back to my suggestion to stay away from mutual funds—particularly if you are investing in a taxable investment account versus your 401(K) plan or an IRA retirement account of some kind. But if you insist on using mutual funds, despite everything I have now outlined for you, at least keep two things in mind: 1. Don't buy at year-end, or you'll be stuck with a tax bill even though you didn't own the fund the whole year. 2. Find a mutual fund that tries to minimize tax exposure. There are "tax-managed" mutual funds, which look to neutralize gains and losses in a given year so that shareholders do not have a tax bill at year-end.

With all these negatives, the concept of investing in individual stocks may be intimidating. I understand that. But there are simple ways to find some good quality stocks. There have been many studies done that show that a monkey throwing darts at a dartboard can pick as many winning stocks as a human. One differentiating factor between a monkey and you is that you have the ability to pull the trigger and sell a stock as necessary. Keeping control of investments for yourself is very important to stay on your financial life path. When I talk to people who have lost money in the past year, there is a universal theme of burying their heads in the sand, and I believe mutual funds are a main culprit in contributing to this lackadaisical attitude. They allow people to think it's easy to give up complete control. While we are forced to use them in a 401(K), unless you are **dollar cost averaging** in those funds, it is hard to see big progress made when we have big upside swings in the market. When you hear the evening news, you do not ever hear a reporter say, "Today XYZ Mutual Fund announced a management change," or "Today XYZ Mutual Fund announced it might declare bankruptcy." But you have heard a reporter declare: "GM ousted its CEO and will be declaring bankruptcy in the coming week." Which of those two examples makes it easier in your conscious life to follow and keep watch over your investments? To me, the ease of which I can find out what's going on with individual companies or even a sector in the overall market is much more appealing than trying to guess what a fund owns, then figuring out if there were any implosions of companies that I own *inside* that fund.

Dollar cost averaging is an investment strategy that requires a consistent investment of the same dollar amount in the same investment, so that over time, more shares are purchased presumably at a lower overall cost.

Myth #11
If you don't know what stocks to buy, just buy an index mutual fund.

On a scale of one to 10, with 10 being the worst, **index funds** probably rank at a 9.5, in my opinion. Most likely, we've all heard the theory that if you do not know which stocks to buy, go with an index fund. Wrong! In the old economy, index funds were viewed as a great tool for long-term investors because the theory was that the entire stock market would keep going up. That's what got us into this mess! Just look at a 10-year rolling return of the S&P 500, including reinvested dividends, and it's easy to conclude that it's a bad idea. Why? Well, unless you hit the right 10 years, you might make nothing in that time. For example, from January 1, 1999 through December 31, 2008 the return would be a compounded rate of -1.4 percent a year! I don't know about you, but I work too hard for my money to see 10 years go down the drain. While the last year or so has been an unusual phenomenon, it's not the only time the market has taken a big tumble. An investor can end up boom or bust just by picking the right or wrong time to invest for that 10-year period in an index fund that follows the broad stock market. But yet, even in the worst markets, my belief is that it is generally possible to find *something* to invest in with a decent return. By sticking to an index fund and having to own stocks from every sector, investors are automatically invested in good, bad, and ugly stocks just because they must own something from every sector of the economy in order to stay "indexed."

An **index fund** is a group of investments that seeks to mimic the returns of a broader market index such as the S&P 500.

Personally, I only want to be in the good sectors that are going to make money. For example, one of the biggest sectors of the S&P 500 is the financials. At times, that one sector accounted for over 20 percent of the S&P 500; in hindsight, there were certain signals that the average person would have recognized. By avoiding that sector, it was possible to shield some of the pain in an investment portfolio as financial stocks got crushed in 2008. But that would only happen if an investor picked where they wanted to be sector by sector, rather than just choosing to be invested in index funds that own something from every sector.

Though simply buying an index fund might be inexpensive, in the long run you are unlikely to prosper. As I write these words I know some economic scholars and investment managers out there will chide me for saying this, but I am just being pragmatic and looking at reality. Think about this: we fell from a Dow Jones Industrial Average of 14,000 points, and it will probably be years before we get to that level again (or at least it *should* be a couple of years). Even though that may be the case, it is very possible to find places to put money that can go up 20 to 40 percent in a year. If you put money into an index fund at a DJIA of 14,000 and left it there, *you would have lost almost 50 percent on your investment in less than six months.* I can assure you it has been a lot quicker for certain stocks and sectors to recover than for the DJIA to get back to 14,000. So unless you are that unwilling to spend some time becoming aware of sectors and industries where there is more upside opportunity than downside, buying an index fund is not a good idea because you give up control to the whims of the market.

There are some good ETFs to help with this. When I know it's a sector I want to be invested in, but don't know enough to pick one stock, I tend to use an ETF rather than a stock. The biotech sector is a good example of this. I might think at some point it is a good place to invest, but I am not knowledgeable enough about medicine to think I can pick a good stock in that sector. In that case, I will attempt to find an ETF that is strictly a basket of biotech stocks. There are many websites to learn even more about ETFs, and several large investment firms that offer a large variety of sector ETFs, which include:

- www.ishares.com
- www.rydex-sgi.com
- www.statestreetspdrs.com

Over the past few years, the ETF industry has really started to boom—and with good reason, given all the negatives with the mutual fund structure. Beyond just creating the ease in which to invest in a sector, ETFs have created a way for the "little guy" to get involved in certain investment categories that only a few years ago would have been impossible to crack— such as gold, currencies, and oil.

There is one cautionary note on ETFs: they are a great alternative to owning individual stocks, but there are some types of ETFs that can be very volatile and risky because they use "leverage." Leverage is often a term associated with lending, but in this case think of it as buying on margin. For example, there are ETFs that are particularly focused on the financial sector. And, there are ETFs that focus on the financial sector, times two or three. That means for every $1 the sector fund goes up or down in a particular day, the leveraged financial sector ETF will go up or down twice or three times as much. Sounds like a great ETF to make money, but it also means increased volatility. Regulators, such as FINRA and the SEC, are now watching these leveraged ETFs more closely to make sure they are being used properly in investor accounts. They are aware that the volatility may make them unsuitable for certain investors. So, before you take the plunge into the world of leveraged ETFs, watch some of them for a while to see how they move versus the underlying market or sector that they are tied to.

Myth #12
Real estate is a great place to invest, but only if you can do it without going into debt.

For centuries, real estate has been one of the best ways to build wealth. Being a landowner has made many people over the ages wealthy beyond their expectations, and over time, it can happen to any of us. One of the oddest things I've heard from one financial expert was the concept of only buying real estate if you can do so without any debt. I believe you have to use debt very conservatively. When buying that house—or even a second or third house—only go forward when you have enough cash to use as a down payment, so that your payments are well within your means, no matter what your financial category is.

I witnessed very sad situations over the last year across every part of the wealth spectrum due to lack of debt conservatism. Even wealthy people, who thought the real estate game would never end, put themselves into homes using way too much debt, thinking they could flip a house to pay for it.

However, the notion that you must have no debt against real estate holdings is wrong. There are benefits to having debt against real estate that are related to tax benefits. If you eventually own enough investment properties, you may be able to qualify as a real estate investor as defined by the tax codes. An accountant can help figure that out. By qualifying for this status, there can be certain benefits to your tax situation, since often investment real estate can be depreciated over time. This means the amount of depreciation could be deducted from your tax liabilities in a given tax year. It also means that rental income from the property can be offset with losses or expenses from maintaining or managing that investment property. My suggestion is to talk to your accountant before buying your first investment property, in order to be aware of how the investment will affect your tax status. Having some options when it comes to tax strategies is something most people who collect a paycheck every week cannot do, but the benefits can be huge. You can make this available to yourself by investing in real estate and using debt wisely.

The point I am trying to stress is that we all want to live the American dream. I believe it is very possible for all of us to do that, even within the confines of a nine-to-five job and without a six-figure paycheck. Many people in this country have bootstrapped their ways to becoming very successful by investing in real estate. By being conservative with how we spend our money, once there is enough accumulated for an emergency, the next step, if it is desirable, is to accumulate enough to become a property owner. Some of us might never get beyond just owning a primary residence, while others might find a way to purchase a rental property that pays its own mortgage. It is just a matter of knowing oneself, thinking through the risks and rewards, and knowing whether it is something that fits into a person's financial life path. We will discuss more about mortgages and mortgage structures a little later.

CHAPTER 4
USING DEBT

I do not believe that debt is an evil thing. Debt has helped many people since the beginning of time become very wealthy. The problem with debt is that it really should be viewed as a tool to create wealth, instead of as a tool to accumulate "stuff." There is a very big difference between using debt to buy a house that has a tangible value versus using debt to buy another new pair of shoes that diminishes in value as soon as you walk out the door of the department store.

The problem over the past year or two has been that as the real estate market has taken such a large downturn, many "experts" have started to swing the pendulum too far to the right and now tell people they should never, ever use debt for anything, including buying a house. Imagine that—just throw thousands of years of how people used debt as a tool to create wealth out the window! I'm here to say once again, *don't buy that bull.*

Myth #13
All debt is bad.

I was amazed to hear one hard and fast rule stated by a leading personal finance expert was that *all* debt and borrowing is bad. Perhaps for some people, they cannot handle using a credit card without abusing it, and in that case, debt is very bad. But when used wisely, debt is in fact a way to create wealth. The three great wealth creators just happen to be the three ways I believe debt can and should be used: 1) real estate debt; 2) entrepreneurial debt; and 3) educational debt.

Statistics show there is a vast differential in net worth between those Americans who own their own home and those that rent. According to statistics from the Federal Reserve, a homeowner's net worth typically is more than 46 times greater than a renter's. The act of home ownership, despite the rocky real estate market we are currently living through, is a wealth creator over time. But let's go beyond that concept and examine these types of debt in detail.

Real Estate Debt

I can tell you dozens of stories about people who have started with very small amounts of money and turned it into millions by investing in real estate. What is at the core of this concept is using borrowed money for a large percentage of the value of the real estate. Banks only make money when they loan it out, so they want to help borrowers when they believe they will get repaid. But borrowing and going into debt have to be taken seriously and must be done prudently. Real estate investors take time to build relationships with their banks over time. Despite everything going on in the banking industry right now, I can assure you that your local community bank wants your business, and they want to build a long-term relationship with you. If you are at all interested in building wealth through accumulating real estate, my suggestion is you go to your local community bank branch and ask the receptionist to speak with the head lender. Introduce yourself to that head lender and explain to him or her that your goal over time is to build a real estate portfolio, and that you'd like to ask a few questions about what the bank's typical loan size is. Other questions to ask the lender are: in which geographic region do they typically make loans, are there any types of properties they will not lend to, and what is the average percentage that bank likes to see its loan customers use as a down payment?

It is important to know that every bank has a "lending limit" that is based on the size of the bank's capital base. Therefore a small bank, i.e., $1 billion in assets, might be able to lend up to $10 million, but it is highly doubtful it has very many loans that are actually at that legal lending limit. As you talk to the head lender, most likely he or she will tell you what the general sweet spot is for the size of investment property loans the lender is willing to underwrite. That person will also probably explain to you the typical loan to value. The concept of "loan to value" or **LTV** is the ratio that every bank will start with to see how much it is willing to lend towards the value of the property in question. This is true whether it's a single-family home, an apartment building, or a strip mall. Every piece of real estate has an appraisal value, which may be more or less than the market price, depending where we are in the economic cycle. Before

DON'T BUY THE BULL

lending money, good bankers make sure the LTV is less than 80 percent on a single-family home—and on investment real estate loans or rental properties, the average bank will want to see an LTV of 70 percent to 75 percent; a percentage that has not changed much, even since banks have tightened their lending standards.

> **Loan to value (LTV)** is the loan amount divided by the value of the property.

But the wealth building part of this only comes into play when debt is used to purchase a piece of real estate that has enough "cash flow" to pay for itself and cover the cost of the loan payments until the bank is repaid. I am talking about using the asset class of real estate to create wealth in the same way you would invest in stocks and bonds, not a primary residence.

This is an example using real numbers that shows the power of smart debt when investing in real estate:

Bob has a good job and has already saved money for emergencies (like all the other personal finance experts tell everyone). Aside from that emergency fund, he has saved $50,000 to invest and wants to do so by investing in real estate. He finds a three-bedroom house in his neighborhood selling for $175,000, and it happens that the house is already occupied with a tenant with a long-term lease. Bob calculates that he can put at least 20 percent down on the house, and the monthly rental income will not only pay his principal and interest mortgage, taxes, and insurance, but also leave a small amount left over for any upkeep or repairs. In his assumptions, he uses a higher interest rate than a standard mortgage rate because he knows that banks generally charge a higher interest rate for investment properties. Bob takes the deal to his local community banker, who he has already met and established a relationship with. Years from now, when Bob's investment property is paid off, essentially Bob will own a property that will likely be worth more than $175,000, and it will have cost him only $50,000 out of pocket. So the return on his cash investment will be over 300 percent or more, if the house goes up in value over time.

Some real estate investors got into trouble in the last few years because they bet that overpriced rental property would continue to increase in value, and they would be able to "flip" at a profit or refinance based on the cash flow of the property. But, here we are, five years later, and the property value has fallen. At the same time, their tenant has closed up shop or moved out, and there is no cash flow on the property. So the important concept to keep in mind if you decide to get involved in the world of real estate investing is to buy only properties that you can afford to make payments on in the event that they become vacant. Also, buy only properties that you want to hold for a long time, not to flip. Ultimately, the amount of time that the real estate is held will decide how the appreciation will come into play. In the example with Bob, he was conservative in his assumptions, knew he could afford the payments if the tenant left, and he had the intent to hold the property for many years in order to realize the long-term appreciation, not just flip it for a small amount quickly.

Investing in real estate in the current environment is starting to look like a much better environment than it has in maybe the last 10 years, according to all the experts I have spoken with. Investors who knew better in the last few years sat on the sidelines, knowing that at some point prices would fall. Those with cash for the 25 percent to 30 percent down payments are in the driver's seat if they can find a property with a solid cash flow that not only pays the loan, but leaves plenty of money for maintenance, repairs, etc. But it is important to do your homework before diving into this—talk to bankers, find statistics on various neighborhoods, and figure out the cost of upkeep on a building.

Over time, the cash flows from rent should pay off the loan on the property, leaving the investor with a great piece of real estate that throws off monthly income. Furthermore, they now own the property, free and clear. The great part of this that can lead to real wealth creation is that the free cash flow from that property can be used to purchase another property. The bank will love this: not only will they have the cash flows from the property they are lending against, but the borrower has another property that has cash flow, too. As the borrower demonstrates responsibility, the bank will begin to trust him or her, allowing for better loan terms over time.

A Note on Debt for Primary Residences

I am a big advocate that people should pay off their primary residence as soon as they possibly can (though some financial experts may disagree with me about this). My reason for this belief is because a primary residence drains you of cash flow every month. The quicker you pay it off, the quicker you'll increase your cash flow (i.e., free cash from your paycheck) to invest or "make work" for you in other productive ways. However, there may be an upside to prolonging mortgage completion. It may boil down to tax consequences for some people. If you're in a higher tax bracket, it may not make much of a difference to write off your mortgage interest against your income. But for someone in a lower tax bracket, it can make all the difference in the world—that debt is therefore good debt because it saves you money in taxes you would otherwise have to pay to Uncle Sam. Over time, your home will hopefully go up in value over many years, and your borrowing to buy the house will ultimately mean more wealth for you and your family in many cases.

Credit Card & Bank Debt

The next type of debt that can be good is not necessarily for everyone. It is for those who have an entrepreneurial spirit and want to become the master of their own destiny by starting their own business. With all the layoffs we keep hearing about every day, many Americans will take this opportunity to go out and attempt to start their own businesses. It can be a very rewarding path to take, but often requires some start-up capital that may go beyond the cash in a bank account.

As I said earlier, most banks want to lend money, but they will only do so when they know they will be repaid. The same goes for going to a bank for a loan to start a business. The reality is the bank's answer will always be no. According to the U.S. Small Business Administration Office of Advocacy, 66 percent of new businesses survive their first two years, 44 percent survive at least four years, and 31 percent survive at least seven years. So, in order to start a business, you really have four choices: use your savings, try getting a loan from the Small Business Administration (www.sba.gov), borrow from friends or family, or use credit cards as your bank. In all these cases, I place a huge warning on the fact that a large percentage of start-up businesses fail. So before you decide to use up your savings, put yourself in credit card debt, or potentially ruin relationships with loved ones, make quite sure that your idea is worth it, and that you have done your research. While I'm not going to list out the number of business concepts I do not think are worth the risk, let me just say simply that retail businesses are the riskiest—the public is fickle and most require you to sell large quantities in order to pay your rent, let alone make a living and a profit. Just do a quick back of the envelope calculation to see if the concept makes sense: how much does the widget cost that you are going to sell? At what price will you sell the widget? Then figure out your costs (cost of goods, salary, rent, insurance, etc.) and divide that monthly cost by the retail cost of your widget. How many widgets will you have to sell to cover that monthly amount? Does that seem feasible, or will it require massive amounts of foot traffic, advertising, or marketing to accomplish? If the answer seems a stretch to accomplish, it's probably not worth the risk. I highly recommend using the tools available on the Small Business Administration website to help with your decision. In addition, get a personal consultation with a member of SCORE (www.score.org), a resource partner to the SBA, which is comprised of thousands of working or retired business executives or entrepreneurs who volunteer their time. His or her experiences can be invaluable to anyone thinking of starting a new business, and it's free!

I believe the sky is the limit for those who have aspirations, and when done in a realistic, calculated manner, using debt to reach those goals can be a wonderful thing. Obviously, borrowing money from friends and family to start a business can be risky, not only for you, but for the lender. When using debt, I would suggest a more traditional route, such as applying for an SBA loan from the government or a local bank. If, by chance, that loan request is denied, do not be disheartened. What most folks do not realize is that there is a method to the madness of banks when they underwrite and turn down a loan. Banks look at a person's financial well-being in its totality, and they crunch the numbers and sometimes determine that the loan payments may be too difficult for that potential borrower. The bank would rather deny you the loan than hurt both parties.

If this situation occurs, I suggest asking the lender why the bank made the decision, and what you need to do in order to be approved the next time. When dealing with debt, denial is usually a delay rather than permanent "no."

I also want to stress here that using credit card debt to fund a start-up business does not mean that I recommend using that same credit card to go out and buy a new blouse or a set of golf clubs, too! It is important simply to think of this credit card as a mini-bank. In today's credit crunch, it may be the only way to fund your new business. The best part about this type of debt is that it is unsecured, which means that your house or other valuable assets do not collateralize it. Given that, the interest rate will be higher than a secured loan (i.e., a mortgage), but since a regular bank loan is not going to be possible, I say, take advantage of the credit line. Use it wisely, and remember to talk to an accountant at tax time since that interest payment will become a tax write-off for your business. Finally, make sure you pay that credit card off as soon as possible, and never make payments late; you absolutely cannot afford to see your credit score suffer in this environment. Credit standards will be tighter now than they were in the past.

Educational Debt

I'm not going to go into details here about the types of loans that are available out there for education. There are entire books written on the topic and many helpful websites. The credit markets are not in great shape, and we do not know when and if they will ever be as liquid as they were prior to 2008. Loans for education are not as easy to come by, though many banks still claim to do private loans for education. In 2008, there were 60 active private lenders that loaned out more than $19 billion. In 2009, 39 lenders dropped out. Those 21 that remain have raised their standards for borrowing. An education, however, is a very important in fulfilling one's aspirations. If you go down this path or finance someone, just make sure that the educational program is completed! How many people know someone who started and stopped school a handful of times only to be left with no degree and a pile of debt? That just sounds insane to me. Not only is the debt a burden, without the degree chances are that paying off that debt will become even more challenging.

Education debt websites include:

- www.salliemae.com
- www.fafsa.ed.gov
- www.ed.gov

Can you tell the common theme in everything I've said here about debt? It can be a very useful and powerful tool when used wisely. You've got to know yourself and your limitations. Be honest with yourself about how much debt you're willing to take on. Hopefully, you've realized that those gurus out there are just giving you the basics. The truth is never that black and white, and I know there are many people out there who want to get to the next step on their financial life path. The key is using the available tools wisely.

Myth #14

It's OK to use PMI.

Private Mortgage Insurance (PMI) is often touted as a way to put potential homeowners into the house of their dreams when they do not have 20 percent to put down, or they do not have enough credit history to make the lender comfortable. Essentially, PMI is extra insurance that a lender wants (and which requires the borrower to pay an extra 1 percent a year in mortgage costs) in order to protect it against a default on the loan. The idea behind it is that the insurance allows the borrower to buy the house if they pay for PMI over a certain amount of time—typically until the borrower's equity in the home has increased to 20 percent or more of the value of the house. Until the PMI is extinguished, the insurance is there to pay back the bank in the event the homeowner defaults. Though laws have been put in place to free buyers from it after the 20 percent threshold is reached, this is easier said than done simply because of the proof needed to show the amount of equity has reached that 20 percent threshold. Typically, it requires more proof of income and verification that the homeowner truly now has 20 percent equity in the house. This often requires a new appraisal. In a difficult real estate market, getting an appraised value that proves a homeowner has 20 percent equity may be difficult.

Private Mortgage Insurance (PMI) is insurance that protects the lender in the case of home loan default.

The bottom line is this: if you cannot get a mortgage without PMI, then you should not be getting that house. Don't let a mortgage broker convince you to use it as part of your loan. Why should you pay for the bank to have insurance on your default? Most Americans have to save money over time in order to garner a down payment on a house. That is the way it has worked for centuries all over the world. Those people who borrowed with less than 20 percent down were more like renters than borrowers, and many of them are now walking away from their homes. This trend is responsible for the almost unstoppable economic death spiral of 2008. Some people may not like to hear this, but the blame of this housing crisis does not completely lie on the shoulders of the mortgage companies that gave out the loans; borrowers who thought there was a shortcut to the American dream also played a role.

I know some will argue that there are ways to avoid PMI such as getting a **wrap around loan**, or a loan for a smaller amount. That way, you have the full 20 percent down to put on your first mortgage and avoid the PMI insurance. That wrap around loan will have to be paid off sooner than 30 years in most cases, but it avoids the PMI. To elaborate, a second loan will not show up to the company underwriting the mortgage as a true mortgage, so it will assume all the money it is collecting as a 20 percent down payment is coming from the borrower (and not the borrowed amount that simply makes it look like they have put 20 percent down). If you insist on buying a house beyond your means, rather than waiting until you save at least 20 percent, then consider the wrap around loan. Again, I really discourage this. Given where real estate values are, it should not be hard to find a home in your price range if you have been saving or have enough home equity in an existing home to trade up or down with enough money to make the down payment.

> A **wrap around loan** is a second loan for a smaller amount, typically no more than 20 percent of the purchase price of a house. It is a loan often used to avoid PMI because it's used by the homebuyer to put the traditional 20 percent down required by the bank in order to avoid PMI.

For me, all of this boils down to making good, solid decisions that will keep you on the right financial life path. Ask yourself: "Can I afford it right now? Do I have enough to put 20 percent down on a house of any cost?" If the answer is yes, then that's the price range you should look to purchase. If that answer is no, then it is still not your time to be a homeowner. Keep saving! Put another way, think of PMI insurance as the equivalent of "insurance" when playing blackjack in a casino. Example: You have a blackjack, and the dealer is showing an ace. Often the casino will give you the opportunity to insure your bet so that even if the dealer ends up with a blackjack, you still win even money on your hand. But those who understand the odds and understand blackjack know this is a sucker's bet. Most of the time, you pay the insurance and end up with a winning hand because the dealer does not turnover blackjack; the player has lost the insurance money they put up anyway. PMI is basically the same thing. It's like flushing money down the toilet. Just don't do it.

Myth #15
Never lease a car.

Part of the reason I wrote this book is because I saw that too many black-and-white answers were being given in personal finance books. Here's the thing: we are all individuals with different situations, and nothing is that black and white for most of us. One of those definitive "rules" I've read frequently is that you should never lease a car. While in many cases leases don't make sense, there are times when they do.

I am a self-professed car junkie. I've gone through many cars in my life, and I've bought cars and leased cars. I have bought used cars, new cars, cars through eBay, and even leased a couple of cars just over the phone from a dealership offering a special lease, thus avoiding that horrible process with a car salesperson. I have learned a lot along the way, and while our logic tells us that a car is just transportation, for some of us, it can be something more. Being the American consumers we are, that's just not good enough. It says something about our style, our personality, and even our status; for some, it is an extension of who we are. This may not be true for everyone, and, frankly, for this economic discussion it does not really matter. What I am trying to say is that in my opinion, it is important to respect yourself by choosing a car that will not only go from point A to point B, but make you happy on the inside, too. It is like buying a new suit for a job interview—it gives you confidence. I am sure many financial gurus will criticize me for saying this, but I'm just living in the real world, and for many people, the choice of vehicle is something that is important. Not everyone drives a sports car and not everyone wants to, but even if your choice is a mini-van, you should feel good about making the decision. Think about what is best for you and what will make you happy. Before you test-drive a car from a used car lot, it's important to think about affordability *and* feeling good about yourself.

With all that said, I want to tackle the concept of buying versus leasing. Let me first say that there is a legitimate choice here for those who are in business for themselves, or own a company. There are a few scenarios when leasing can make sense, such as when you're self-employed or a business owner. The lease payment is considered a pre-tax expense when the car is used for business purposes, which is a tax write-off. If you fall into one of these scenarios, I still suggest talking to your accountant first before pulling the trigger on a lease. Keep in mind there are often limits to mileage on a lease agreement, and any overages can get expensive enough to offset tax benefits from tax write-offs.

This is one financial decision that I believe requires a thorough examination of the tax implications before moving forward in one direction or another. I am not advocating buying a more expensive car because the lease payment will mean a lower payment for a more expensive vehicle. I am looking purely at the numbers—assuming you've already picked out the correct vehicle for your situation and now are deciding to buy or lease. A car loan does not get treated the same way as a lease; the car is depreciated over time, and it generally requires using a formula to calculate how much of the car loan can be devalued. It is generally going to be less effective for tax planning than a car lease would be, and with the state of the U.S. budget deficit, I suspect future tax reforms will leave business owners in a bit of a tax pinch, seeking ways to help save a few pennies at tax time.

I am an advocate of *never buying a new vehicle.* Visit any number of auto-industry websites, such as Edmunds.com or Kelley Blue Book (KBB.com) and just check out the price of a new car and then price that car's used model from two years ago. It is amazing how much the value of every car drops in just the first 12 to 24 months. Even if you can afford a new car, why do it? With all the dealer certification programs available now, it's possible to get an amazing deal on a slightly used car with low miles and come with all kinds of warranties and certifications. Of course I say all of this with a note of caution to do plenty of homework before buying a used vehicle. Check out Edmunds.com for a list of "best bets" on used cars. Also consider spending a few dollars to buy a CARFAX report to make sure the car you're buying has a clean history and title with no previous history of flood, collision, etc. Though there is always a small amount of risk buying a used car, you can save anywhere from 10 percent to 40 percent just by looking at a model that is only a couple of years old. Paying for that new car smell just isn't worth it to me.

Myth #16
Interest-only mortgages are insane.

There are a number of ways that people with lumpy income or are in business for themselves can use various financial tools to manage their monthly cash flow needs. The decision on a lease versus purchase of a car is just one way to do that. But there are others as well. Just because your income may fluctuate from time to time due to bonuses or less hourly work doesn't mean you can't be a homeowner. It just takes using debt in the right way, using the right type of debt structure.

Interest-only mortgages can be a good tool for certain people. One of the most interesting aspects of the housing market crisis has been the criticism of all mortgage structures that are not conventional 30-year fixed mortgages. In our society, people are compensated very differently, so how can the same mortgage structure work for everyone? A one-size mortgage does not fit all, so these financial experts should stop making blanket statements about mortgage structures.

I do believe there were real issues related to mortgage underwriting standards, and that the wrong mortgage structures were given to the wrong borrowers. However, as you look at your own life, keep your options open about which structure works best for you, even in this environment. Essentially, an interest-only mortgage means paying the interest on your mortgage every month, not the principal. You stay flexible in order to pay down the balance of the mortgage faster. For example, someone who has a career in sales might get a bonus check once a year. He or she can use that bonus to pay down the mortgage. The beautiful part of this structure is that sending in that extra check will result in a lower payment the following month because that extra check decreases the principal balance left on the mortgage, making this a great option for people with income that can be "lumpy" or irregular and people with consistent bonuses. In these situations, you may be able to pay down a house very quickly.

Some will try to use these mortgages as way to get into a house that is more than they could afford with a traditional principal and interest type of mortgage. I would strongly discourage this. Remember, these interest-only mortgages do adjust—they will typically start out as a one-, three-, five-, seven-, or 10-year fixed mortgage that becomes adjustable, so lock in as long as you possibly can on that interest-only rate. That is how many people got in trouble over the past couple of years—they thought they'd be in the house only a year or two, so only took a short-term, interest-only loan that had a very low teaser interest rate (therefore a low payment every month). As the real estate market turned, it became difficult to sell a house *and* the refinance market dried up. That meant bigger payments since the teaser period was over, and the real estate bubble started to burst. If you go down this path, remember to give yourself as much time as possible and to lock in for as long as you can. Be sure you are committing yourself to paying it down.

In summary, the interest-only mortgage can be a great tool for people who have an extra lump of cash; it forces people to pay off a mortgage quickly by allowing them to pay down the principal, while the conventional 30-year fixed mortgage ties you up for 30 years. Some may not have a choice—and that's okay. It is important to know which suits your financial needs the best. In general, just assume if you have a job that is stable and does not include fluctuations in income, that a traditional mortgage is probably the best mortgage for you.

Myth #17
Never borrow using an adjustable rate loan.

One of the interesting things about the real estate cycle is its effect on interest rates. There are certain times when it is easier to look out over the horizon and predict that in three or five years we'll have higher interest rates than we have now, or, conversely, that in three to five years interest rates will be lower.

Here we are in the wake of a financial disaster that would have been worse without the fast thinking of Chairman Bernanke and the Federal Reserve, who took interest rates to zero. So, in essence, rates can't get any lower than they are right now. When using an adjustable rate mortgage, generally they are tied to an index (such as prime rate, **LIBOR**, or **CMT**) plus some spread over that index. Three years ago, if you borrowed using an adjustable rate loan with a three-year lock up, your payments have probably adjusted downward. In the short term, it costs less, but five years from now, the payment will go back up because the interest rates will climb once again. I can say this because it is just applying common sense. The Federal Reserve cannot keep interest rates at zero for a long period of time without introducing the risk of inflation into the economy. Therefore, once it sees that we are solidly on a path of economic growth, traditionally, this is when it will begin to raise interest rates again. That will happen in this situation, although *when* that increase in rates starts is still anybody's guess. But once it starts, payments on adjustable mortgages will inevitably start to go back up.

INTEREST RATE BENCHMARKS

LIBOR is the London Inter Bank Offering Rate. Visit http://www.investopedia.com/terms/l/libor.asp for details.

CMT is the Constant Maturity Treasury rate. Visit http://www.investopedia.com/terms/c/cmtindex.asp for details.

This is where things can get dangerous by making the wrong decisions. If considering using an ARM (Adjustable Rate Mortgage), my advice is to lock in for as long you possibly can. Try to envision your life within the next few years or longer. If it's a sure thing that you won't be in that house a couple years down the road, then maybe the ARM is a good product. But if the plan is to stay in that home for life, then this is not a good mortgage structure for you—unless using an interest-only loan allows you pay it down quickly. Locking in to a rate for the long term is something that will give a long-term homeowner the solace of mortgage payment stability.

I think many people forget that their ability to plan their financial life path takes some time, and asking hard questions before making big financial decisions is very important. No one has a crystal ball. But at least mapping out where you want to be down the road will give you some peace and a sense of direction. No one else can do this for you.

CHAPTER 5
LIFE & MONEY DECISIONS

Decisions you make about investing and debt aren't the only critical choices that can shape how your financial situation turns out as you approach retirement. Your spouse or partner can be an important factor, especially if you're a saver and your mate is a spender! Or, as another example, you both may have different thoughts on how to teach children about money.

Some of my advice on this is nothing more than common sense. Most of what I have to say is straight, honest talk. And most importantly, all of what I say here ultimately comes back to listening to your inner voice in order to keep on track.

Myth #18
Never marry anyone who insists on a prenup.

Apparently there are some religion-based financial experts out there. The notion of having no prenuptial agreement is just insane! During my one year in law school long ago, I had a contracts class. My professor, who was a worldly gentleman, stood in front of us one day when we reached the section about marriage contracts, and proclaimed that he if ever heard that one of his students got married without a prenuptial agreement, he would come find them and wring their neck for being so stupid! After hearing such strong advice, I realized how right he was. While I respect religion, I think that we should also live by the separation of church and state when it comes to our money. I'm not going to get into the concepts of tithing and giving money to charity—both concepts can be very fulfilling for those who wish to embark on them in a way that it does not hurt their financial life path. But, taking a step away from those "charity" concepts, I would prefer to take a more a defensive posture when it comes to financial decisions. Call me cynical, but considering that the divorce rate in this country remains at 50 percent, according to a report published in 2006 by the U.S. Census Bureau, I think that to ignore the odds of a marriage ending in a divorce would be the equivalent of hiding under a blanket. Since one of the main tools of staying on the right financial life path is awareness of one's surroundings, I would suggest looking at the facts.

The lack of an agreement upfront, whether it is a marital prenuptial or a cohabitation agreement for a same sex couple, is like playing Russian roulette. The odds are only 50–50 that the relationship will make it to the Silver Anniversary stage, so, don't risk it. I am not suggesting the agreement protects one part more than the other—the purpose is to protect both parties and to be fair and clear about what each party expects and is entitled to if the marriage/partnership is dissolved.

This is a contract like any other. In business, when doing a merger deal, there is always a break-up clause. This clause simply states the penalty if one party walks away from the other and vice versa. The marriage contract should work the same way. If asking your soon-to-be spouse about his or her willingness to sign a prenup sounds too difficult, my advice is to get over it! The difficulty of having that conversation is nothing compared to the legal bills you may have to deal with some day, not to mention the heartache over deciding (with someone you detest at that point) who keeps the house, the furniture, or even the dog. Talk to someone you know who has been through a divorce and did not have a prenup. Chances are, they regret not having a prenup to rely on at the end of the relationship because it would have made the process of getting divorced "cleaner."

If religious upbringing still weighs on your conscience or just the concept of a prenup sounds too unromantic, consider this. A prenup is a prophylactic. It may never be necessary because things may go very well. But unless you can answer in the affirmative to any of the following questions, think twice about entering marriage or a committed relationship without one:

- Would you stay together in a violent or abusive situation?
- If your spouse or partner cheated on you, would you stay married?
- If one of you decided to move to Antarctica some day and the other did not want to, would you stay married?

If, after those kinds of scenarios, the answer is still a yes, then that is your decision. My goal here is to make a case for reality and pragmatism, particularly when it comes to keeping a financial life path. Of course, consulting with an attorney about a prenup is very important. If you happen to be someone with a respectable amount of assets before getting married, or you know you may inherit a large sum of money in the future, there may be some special considerations for you to discuss with your lawyer in order to protect yourself. There is nothing wrong with being generous with a spouse or life partner, but do so in a way that is smart by getting the objective advice of a lawyer.

Myth #19
The $100 a month you give to your kids for little indulgences is not worth it—buy a life insurance policy instead.

A life without any simple pleasures does not really seem like a fulfilled life at all. In order for children to know how to interact with the world, how to understand the value of dollar, and how to work towards attaining goals, we must teach them. And along the way, part of being a child is being allowed to have a childhood. Ask the children living in parts of the world where they are forced to work at the age of six or seven, who are helping to support their families. I am sure they would give anything to have one day—or even one hour—when they could just go have a scoop of ice cream.

One of the things that I believe makes this country great is the respect we have for our children and their need to grow up in a happy environment. We have child labor laws for a reason, so, when I hear personal finance experts dolling out advice about making a kid sacrifice a bit of their childhood so that parents can buy life insurance policies, it makes me cringe. Even Jane, though homeless for a period of time, realized the importance of finding a way to give her daughter the opportunity to be a child. It is possible to do that without spending a lot of money—there are free concerts, free museums, and many other community events out there that cost nothing. Beyond free, spending a few dollars a month for an ice cream cone or a Happy Meal are activities that I guarantee will create cherished memories for a child that are important.

Clearly, there are excesses, and many children have gotten completely spoiled. Since don't I have any kids, I can only tell from observation that many parents seem to build their lives around their children nowadays, instead of the reverse. I watch shows such as MTV's *Sweet Sixteen* and want to vomit by the end. It is just so sad how parents can raise children with such materialistic values. It's one thing to want a Range Rover—work for it hard enough and anything is possible. It is another thing to have one handed to you at the age of 16, "just because mommy and daddy love you." When I asked Jane how she felt about this topic even she agreed with me: there has to be a fine line between keeping on the right financial path and allowing for life's simple (and inexpensive) little pleasures for a child to develop and enjoy childhood. There is a way to succeed at this—it just takes a bit of good old-fashioned parenting. My niece and nephew, for example, have two beautiful little children. When we take them to the amusement park every summer, my nephew will tell his kids that the maximum number of ride tickets that the park will sell to little boys and girls is 10. That way, the kids can enjoy themselves, and my nephew saves his budget by putting a reasonable limit on the kids in a way that is simple for them to understand. He is putting himself through college right now, but he still manages to find a way to make sure his children have happy childhoods without sacrificing the necessities.

Unfortunately, I think parents who fail at putting limits on how they reward their children risk the long-term success their children may be able to realize in life. If everything is handed to them as a child, they will grow used to this, and as adults it will be harder to function in the real world where people aren't so friendly and generous. So while parents who can afford to give a child everything may think it's an act of generosity and shows love, it may, ultimately, prove to be a destructive act.

The key to this is setting boundaries. As I said earlier, present youths are controlling parents. In order to stay on this all-important financial life path, which your children have no clue about, it is important for you to maintain your authority by setting limits on activities that cost a lot of money if your financial situation is tight. Yes, clearly spending money on precautions, such as a life insurance, is important, but so are non-monetary things, like a childhood. But even if finances are under control, there is nothing wrong with imposing frugality on your children in order to keep them from becoming like the spoiled rotten kids on *Sweet Sixteen*. If the money is there, and they are at an age where it makes sense to give them chores to do, have them earn the right to do more than what your original boundaries allow. Throw them a few bucks for helping you around the house. Hard work is what this country was founded on, and teaching kids about the balance between work and play early on in life is something I know they will appreciate when they have a family of their own. And then take it a step further, just to make sure they are learning good spending and saving habits. Review how and what they are doing with that allowance money until you are sure they have been trained to do a bit of both. One note of caution about this: *do not put too much pressure on your children!* I have a close friend that was given a checkbook when she was a teenager. While that sounds very generous of her parents, it was extremely stressful for her because they expected her to show them a balanced checkbook every single month. That is a lot of pressure to put on a child or adolescent. However you plan on teaching this lesson, try to do it in a way that is age appropriate.

Myth #20
Parents should always put their own financial health before their children's education.

I have a strong work ethic—something that most people my age pride themselves on having. As a child of the '80s, we are the last generation that had to struggle through school using a basic calculator, do research in a library using the Dewey Decimal System, and perhaps even watch television in black and white. While these basics still exist, they are antiquated given all the other "high tech" options available these days. So children growing up now have a lot more options available to them—maybe this is why so many kids are diagnosed with ADD?

As I entered the work force and progressed in my career, I started observing the lack of work ethic of those even a few years younger than me. At first I thought maybe I was just getting old—but then I started comparing my notes with others my age and older. It seemed to be a general consensus that the young generations have been raised to be much more self-centered and focused on instant gratification. While technology has admittedly made younger generations grow up in an "instant gratification" world, where information can be found with the stroke of a couple of buttons and the latest video game can be downloaded in a few seconds, I still believe it has to do with parenting and upbringing. As a result, they have quickly achieved a reputation for not being desirable workers because they are not willing to put in the hard work necessary to learn their trade and move up the ladder.

Raising children is not an easy task. In fact, I've heard even some of the best and brightest business executives say their hardest job in life was being a good parent, not running a billion-dollar company. I respect that. Yet, I believe there has to be a way to continue having a life and still raise a well-rounded, self-sufficient child.

I have heard a couple of personal finance experts say that parents should explain their financial situations to their children. Imagine sitting down your five-year-old and telling him or her you have only enough money for them to eat one meal a day for the next two weeks. That's a great way to put the fear of God into a small child and leave permanent damage. That I know because of what I have witnessed with Jane and her daughter. Even if it's not an extreme situation like that, there comes a point when it becomes too much information. My experience with Jane taught me this, as she has struggled to get her daughter to have a sense of normalcy after being traumatized during their time spent being homeless. Think back to your own childhood—did your mom and dad sit you down and have adult-like conversations about household finances with you? Probably not, although I am sure on some level a parent probably told you "no, we have to wait till Christmas for that new toy." That's basically the same thing as saying the money isn't there for the new toy, but getting that message across in such a way that it does not make the child feel that his or her world is unsafe. As you grew older, of course, the tone and details explained may have increased. Along the way, you may have been taught that with hard work and doing chores around the house, you would make a little money in an allowance and be able to use some of that for the extras in life you may have wanted— like that package of Sea Monkeys in the back of the latest *Superman* comic book. As teenage years approached, you became conscious of the world around you. Whether or not your parents would be able to afford footing the bill for your higher education probably became more obvious to you.

Secondary School Education

The importance of a good education becomes more and more intense with each day, but college is just too expensive. For the average family, even state-funded universities are becoming unaffordable. While I believe it is important to save the moment a child is born for his or her education, it might not be possible to save enough to cover all costs. I personally believe you should do the best you can—saving what you can to give your child the best shot to start off adult life debt-free, while putting money aside for your retirement and financial emergencies.

I have seen even modest income families assist their children with school because they watched their expenses. This includes the basic techniques many are using to recover following the stock market crash. Many are eating dinner at home more, staying closer to home for vacations, and saving money. My hope is this newfound practicality is getting us back to a place where my generation and those before me, used to live. The lowering of expectations for lifestyle is not such a bad thing for children now, and in the end, I believe, it will help parents get their kids the better opportunities and bigger savings for important things.

Myth #21
Cosigning on a loan is OK to help someone out.

It's difficult to hear the sad stories of people losing jobs and getting down on their luck financially. It can happen to any of us. This is part of the normal ebbs and flow of our economy—peaks and valleys, which mean sometimes there are times of greater prosperity. Those of us who are big-hearted want to help. Many times this help comes in the form of a loan—and the need for a cosignatory.

At first blush, you may think that it is not a big

deal to cosign on a loan since your loved one will be responsible for the payment. Typically, people who need a cosigner either have bad credit or no credit. The bank does not think they are a good credit risk, so why should you? At first, everything seems fine, and then after a few months, your loved one forgets to make a payment. The bank will then start calling you, as the responsible party, to remind you that the payment is due. So you have to call and tell your loved one to send in the payment. This creates an awkward situation for you. Let's say things get worse—and the bank calls again. This time the banker tells you that there are three payments that are past due. This means the bank now wants you to pay up—they are not going to wait for the actual borrower to send in the money. Since you're the cosigner, you are legally responsible. What if you can't afford to pay someone else's bill? Well... Bam! Look no further than your credit report and you will see that now your credit score is much lower than the last time you checked.

Now you have jeopardized your financial life path just because you wanted to do something nice. Why is it so bad when your credit score drops? It means possibly not getting credit for something you really need. It can also mean having to pay a much higher interest rate on a loan if you can get credit, and unfortunately, this new lower credit score will stick with you for years. The solution is, of course, to tell anyone who ever asks you to have the honor of cosigning that, as a policy, you long ago decided you would not do that. However, if they need help in some other way, you are happy to help them—be a reference, help them financially with a down payment—whatever you feel you can do without jeopardizing your financial life path, while being a kind and generous person to someone you care about.

Myth #22
Helping others and giving to charity is always a wonderful and fulfilling experience.

At the start of this book I mentioned that part of my inspiration revolved around my helping a woman and her daughter who found themselves in a situation of homelessness. I have always been profoundly moved by homelessness because at my core, I believe that any one of us could end up that way if we made a couple of wrong decisions along the way. To me, this means reaching out and giving a helping hand to someone who needs it. But I took a real chance in what I did. And so, I'd have to say, while I think it worked out in my case, I cannot say that will always be the case.

The bottom line—don't do it. My reasons for advising against helping others outside of an organizational structure are not only financial or tax related; there are reasons that are more difficult to quantify in terms of dollars and cents. Of course, there are so many positives in charitable giving. According to the author of *The Healing Power of Doing Good*, Allan Luks, there are both physical and emotional positives in helping others; a heightened sense of well-being, relief from insomnia, and even a strong immune system. And there are so many causes that need help—thousands of causes are in need of financial assistance and volunteers.

The reason for my insistence on getting involved in charitable giving *only* within a charitable organization is because that should ensure that there is some amount of screening being done; meaning the check you are writing is going specifically to the cause in which you intend it to. It also should guarantee that the charity you are working with has an infrastructure in place to ascertain that those being helped are on the right path and using the aid in order to help him or herself improve. It's a difficult thing to admit, but for those of us who are hard working and try to see the good in everyone and everything, it is not always the best way to approach charitable giving. On some level, many of the people who need help from charities are, in fact, either emotionally or mentally unstable. They might need a special kind of assistance that the average, untrained professional cannot possibly imagine or know how to give. This is why getting involved with a charitable organization is the best way to proceed. It makes it easier to give when you know that trained professionals are involved and the recipients receive the kind of help they really need—both financial (from you and other donors) as well as the other assistance that only trained professionals, such as social workers, are qualified to give.

From a tax perspective, there are several things to keep in mind. First, if you itemize your taxes, you can claim your donations as a deduction—but be prepared to produce documentation to back up your claims of donations. If you donate more than $250, make sure you get a receipt because you will have to use that to prove your donation in order to take the deduction. And, if what you are donating is *an item* with a value more than $5,000, you may need to have documentation to prove the market value/appraised value is in fact worth more than $5,000. If you find yourself in a really charitable mood—keep in mind that from a tax write-off perspective, donations cannot be more than 50 percent of your adjusted gross income or 20 to 30 percent in some cases. Check with your accountant to make sure. Any amount donated over 50 percent of your adjusted gross income can be carried over for up to five more future tax years.

I would recommend that the best place to start is to determine what type of cause you have an interest in. There are some terrific websites to help sort this out:

- www.charitynavigator.org
- www.bbb.org
- www.charitywatch.org

After doing some background checking on your potential charities and visiting all of their websites, the only thing left to do is to decide. This, of course, means you will have to listen to your inner voice to do what "feels right" to you. This is something that you can do with your spouse or your children—it is never too young to get kids involved in giving to others.

Myth #23
You can do all this on your own.

I believe every person here on earth is born with a special gift. Some of us might be born with natural ability to play sports. Others of us might have a good ear for learning foreign languages. I consider myself blessed that my gift from above is a knack for stock picking and a natural feel for the stock market. While I have had years of training and schooling in financial topics, that is not all that it takes to be good at being a professional investor. I think there's a "secret sauce" to it that is unexplainable. Fortunately for me, my life path has allowed me utilize this gift in my career. I am able to make a living doing something that I enjoy—yes, I know I am a bit of a nerd. But not everyone has this talent. Most people do not have the time to watch their investments or do things like draft their own legal documents. My conclusion then, of course, is to get help! Reading up on basics to understand personal finance topics is a great idea—and some of these ideas you can implement for yourself, such as budgeting, savings, and figuring out what type of mortgage structure to use. But when it comes to other areas, a "DIY" mentality needs to be implemented very carefully, or you could make things worse for your financial life path. After reading this book, I think the average reader understands that there are lots of nuances to investing, familiar to professionals who have been doing it for a while, that most people have no idea about.

Since the stock market crashed in 2008, I have had

more people tell me in a cocktail-setting conversation that they are turning their money over to the hands of professionals to manage for them. They realized they could not do it on their own, but unfortunately, that realization came after they lost a boat load of money in the stock market. I think many people who were formerly of that "DIY" mentality now accept the fact that managing their life (job and family), along with their financial life without some help, is just too monumental for them to do. There's just not time for most people to watch their investments, and they really don't understand enough about the markets to do it really well.

We are not in the same world we were a year ago. Some people have already resigned themselves to this conclusion and have taken steps to get back on the right financial path by asking for help from an investment professional. Finding the right investment professional might take a little bit of effort and quite a few interviews. But do it! Please do not bury your head in the sand and continue to think all the investments you have that are down 50 percent are going to go back up eventually over time. They might not—you might be in the wrong investments for this new world we live in. While I am not trying to scare anyone, I am trying to lay down some realities. Those self-directed online brokerage firms that tell you that with their "research reports" and low trading commissions you can do this on your own—don't believe it. If you do, call me when you're in a business meeting at 1:30 in the afternoon one day and the market takes an 800-point dive in two hours without your knowledge. Then, your portfolio drops down 25 percent because you weren't around to sell when things started to look like they were getting ugly. That is the value of having an investment professional on your team—just like dealing with a doctor who looks after your physical health; an investment professional is the person that looks after the health of your financial life path in conjunction with you.

It's not to say that all people in the investment industry are created equal because they are not. How and where to find someone right for you and your financial life path? I think the best place to find someone is through your own network of contacts. Ask friends and family or coworkers who they trust and use, then focus in on the referrals that are not stockbrokers, but financial advisors. A stockbroker is only a salesperson, and the client still has to be part of that decision-making process on whether or not the stock or bond the sales person is selling is something you should be buying. My preference is to use a financial advisor or money manager who is actually deciding for clients what the right investment choices are, based on goals and a risk profile. They have discretion over the account to make those choices. Obviously, that requires some trust on the part of a client. The next step will be to interview a few of those referrals. Keep in mind, choosing to move forward and hire a financial advisor or investment advisor does not mean losing consciousness of your own financial life or investments!

My advice in describing what quality I would look for would be someone who has a pleasant disposition and who you like as a person. More importantly, you need someone who is very intelligent and has been through a couple of ugly markets—i.e., didn't just get into this business a year or two ago, but has at least a decade of experience behind them. It is this experience that will help them keep a cool head in stressful situations—not run for the hills (or the garbage can to puke) when the markets get extremely volatile. Other areas of focus when trying to find that right investment advisor are things like education and training. As far as business practices—no one wants to end up in a **Madoff-like Ponzi scheme**—there are some very simple questions to ask in order to mitigate that sort of risk.

- Does the investment advisor firm have custody of client assets?
- Does the investment advisor firm have to trade

with only a particular brokerage firm?

- Is the firm associated or owned by a brokerage firm? If so, is that brokerage firm self-clearing, i.e., they settle their own transactions in house and print their own statements and trade confirmations?

If the answer to any of these three questions is yes, then run for the door. While that doesn't mean this a dishonest advisor, it does mean that the business is set up in such a way operationally that there is a risk that clients could find themselves in a Madoff-like situation. It is that simple. Move on to another advisor.

BERNIE MADOFF

Bernard Madoff was the man convicted in 2009 for the biggest Ponzi scheme in history by stealing billions of dollars from investment clients. His performance returns for people were very high for years. But yet, it was discovered these returns were all manufactured using computer programs, and no trading had ever taken place in people's accounts. Every statement and trade confirmation sent to his clients was a fake. Unfortunately, it was impossible for the average person to know this without having asked certain questions.

If, after exhausting your own internal network of referrals the right financial advisor or money manager still eludes you, then try the Internet. Here are just a few websites to help with your search:

- www.wiseradvisor.com

- www.moneymanager.com

- www.advisorhunt.com

But this is not the end of your quest to build a good team of advisors who can help you with your financial life path. Two other types of professionals to consider forming relationships with are accountants and lawyers.

Accounting is something we most often equate with taxes. That's definitely a big reason why it is important to have a good accountant. Regardless of how much money you make, an accountant can help you keep as much money in your pocket rather than overpay Uncle Sam. They can also help you look at big-ticket economic decisions with an eye towards what is best from a tax perspective. I think a lot of people don't do this—and end up leaving money on the table for themselves or paying extra in taxes just because they did not look at things with an eye towards what the tax consequences would be if they chose a different route. For example, when deciding about whether or not to rent or buy a home—it may not be a question of what you can afford. The question may be a decision about monthly cash flow out of your paycheck. If the decision is between buying a house with 20 percent down payment and end up with $1,200 per month mortgage versus rent a house with a $1,200 rent, your accountant can run the numbers and tell you whether it's a good idea or not from a tax-savings perspective. As with finding a financial advisor, talk to friends and family first to get some referrals. And meet a few of them. Unfortunately, accountants can have a tendency to make anyone's eyes glaze over when talking to them—even for people with a head for numbers like me. So if you interview an accountant and he starts explaining something to you and your head starts spinning as a result, then maybe that's a sign he does not speak the same language as you.

I have one other caveat about finding a good accountant. Use your accountant only for accounting matters—not investments. Investments, of course, should be left in the hands of your investment advisor. In the past few years, there was a growing trend in the accounting industry of CPAs getting licensed to sell investment products. Sounds good in theory, right? After all, if they are good with numbers ,then that means they must be good at investments.

The problem is, most accountants I know were not trained to pick investments—and they don't have the time to watch investments if they are doing their primary job of being an accountant. Try calling your accountant during tax season. It's next to impossible to get a phone call back unless it's something urgent. How on earth could they possibly follow the markets then, if they are buried up to their ears in tax filings for their clients? So what often happens is that your account gets put on autopilot into a bunch of mutual funds—and it may not be looked after as closely as if you had hired an investment advisor to manage your investments.

There is one more person to add to your list of experts for your financial life path—a good lawyer. Again, it is not about how much money you have or don't have. Even if you don't have a lot of money to spend on legal fees, you will need some legal advice or need a legal document drafted from time to time. Protect yourself and spend the few dollars, even use an online service. The downside risk by not protecting yourself could seriously derail your financial life path. There are ways to keep legal fees to a minimum, depending on the circumstances. For example, I already discussed a few topics in this book related to legal help, like marriage and divorce. A prenup is something needed and a lawyer can draft that for you. Or, in this instance you can use any number of legal websites to help you draft the document. I have found a few good legal websites depending on the circumstance:

- www.legalzoom.com—for general legal documents
- www.legaldocs.com—for general legal documents
- www.mycorporation.com—for incorporating
- www.legaleinstein.com—for wills
- www.completecase.com—for divorce

If your circumstance is more complicated or you have the extra cash to spend on a top-notch lawyer, then by all means, go for it. One bit of advice in this regard, however. Not every lawyer is good for every situation. Save time and money by hiring the right lawyer. That doesn't just mean find a divorce lawyer for a divorce. There are lots of good divorce lawyers—but how messy or nasty do you think your divorce may get? If the answer is you think it could get really ugly, then you may need a pit-bull lawyer who is aggressive and acts as your personal shield. If, on the other hand, the divorce is amicable, then hiring a lawyer with a very calm, even-keeled demeanor may be the right tactic in order to keep things very civil during the process. This concept every situation—whether it's something that will enter a courtroom or not.

Conclusion

The intent of this book was not to be just another personal finance book. My goal was to enlighten and debunk some of the common myths I've seen out there in a lot of other personal finance books. At the end of the day, the success of any financial life path depends only on the individual. Hopefully, some of the information in this book can help put the tools in readers' hands to stay on the right track. The next time a personal finance guru gives you a definitive "do" or "don't" regarding some sort of financial decision, keep in the back of your mind the phrase, *don't buy the bull!* We're still in for a wild ride for many years. I hope this book has given you a road map and maybe even get to your goals a little sooner.